recordist and record label owner. He has recorded Yanomamö Indian shamanistic music in Amazonas, broadcast music talks for BBC Radio Three, recorded and produced a wide variety of records (from Prince Far I to Frank Chickens). He is co-editor of *Collusion* magazine. He has recently written for *The Face*, *Black Echoes*, *Rock Session* and the *Sunday Times*, and is currently collaborating with film-maker Jeremy Marre on a major television series for Channel Four on British music.

'David Toop rolls away the stones to uncover a hidden world of B Boys, Hip Hoppers and Planet Rockers, where time is caught in a frantic loop, and where taste is a matter of "if it fits, use it". Meet all the leading Electro Rappers including Africa Bambaataa and Grandmaster Flash, and discover the pioneers of the most potent new sound of the Eighties.'

Charlie Gillett, author,
The Sound of the City

'David Toop has put together a rap attack of stories and fact which take the reader hip hopping across the "street-wave" which represents rap music today. *The Rap Attack* is "down by law" for understanding the roots of the rappers in America – past, present and future.'

Gary Byrd, DJ,
Sweet Inspirations

David Toop

THE RAP ATTACK

African jive to New York hip hop

Rap photographs: Patricia Bates

Pluto Press

First published in 1984 by Pluto Press Limited,
The Works, 105a Torriano Avenue, London NW5 2RX
and Pluto Press Australia Limited,
PO Box 199, Leichhardt,
New South Wales 2040, Australia.

Second impression 1985

Every effort has been made to locate the copyright owners of the material quoted in the text. Omissions brought to our attention will be credited in subsequent printings. Grateful acknowledgement is made to the following publishers: Clappers Music Inc. for *How We Gonna Make the Black Nation Rise?*, A Nubyhahn/S Lynn © 1980; Profile Records for *Beat Bop*, Rammelzee Vs. K-Rob, © Protoons, Inc. 1983; Tommy Boy Records for *Play That Beat Mr DJ*, MC Globe/Whiz Kid, © Tee Girl Music T-Boy Music 1983; Carlin Music Corp for *The Jam*, L Graham, © 1975; Intersong Music for *Get On the Good Foot*, J Brown, F Wesley, J Mims, © 1973.

Cover designed by Dennis Morris

Set by Wayside Graphics, Clevedon, Avon
Printed in Great Britain by Photobooks (Bristol) Limited
Bound by W. H. Ware & Sons Limited,
Tweed Road, Clevedon, Avon

British Library Cataloguing in Publication Data
Toop, David
The rap attack: African jive to New York hip hop
1. Music, Popular (Songs, etc.) — History and criticism
I. Title
780′.42 ML3470

ISBN 0-86104-777-X

Contents

Acknowledgements / 7
Prerap / 8
1. **On the corner** / 12
2. **Doo-wop hip hop** / 22
3. **African jive** / 29
4. **Beat bop** / 36
5. **Sister brother rapp** / 47
6. **Uptown throwdown** / 56
7. **Raptivity in captivity** / 78
8. **Version to version** / 104
9. **Tough** / 116
10. **Whiplash snuffs the candle flame** / 126
11. **Wotupski, bug byte?** / 146

Words up! Glossary by Monica Lynch / 158
Lightning swords of death One hundred Rap Attack 12-inch singles and a selection of albums / 161
Bibliography / 164
Index / 165

Acknowledgements

I would like to thank all the people who generously gave me their time and knowledge in interviews and conversations: Bobby Robinson (Enjoy), Grandmaster Flash and his minder Kevin, Afrika Bambaataa, G.L.O.B.E. and Mr Biggs (Soul Sonic Force), Amad (Shango), KK Rockwell and Lil Rodney Cee (Double Trouble/The Deuce), Jimmy Castor, Aaron Fuchs (Tuff City), Kurtis Blow, Paul Winley, The Fearless Four, Dennis Weeden, Ms D.J., Davy DMX, Spoonie Gee, Gary Byrd, Mr Magic, The Force MDs, Lotti Golden and Richard Scher (Warp 9), Arthur Baker, Dr Ice and Kid Kangol (UTFO), Ecstacy (Whodini), Bill Laswell (Material), Pumpkin, Fab Five Freddy, Gary Simms (manager – Soul Sonic Force), Vincent Davies (Vintertainment Records), Bill Scarborough (Sound of New York), Lister Hewan Lowe (Clappers), Monica Lynch (Tommy Boy), Anthony Giammanco (Reelin' and Rockin'), Cory Robbins (Profile), Celluloid Records, Spring Records, Roger Trilling, Tony Heilbut.

I would also like to thank all the people who gave me valuable information, loaned records and gave support and encouragement at crucial moments: Sue Steward (who first brought back news of Flash and the Funky Four in the early days of rap on record), Stuart Cosgrove (who read the manuscript and offered many useful suggestions), Steve Beresford, Steven Harvey, Matthew Wright, Nick Kimberley, Andrew Brenner, Kazuko Hohki, Hector, Dave Hucker, Graham Lock, Hannah Charlton, Black Echoes, The Face, Compendium Bookshop, Rhythm Records, Ray's Jazz Records, Collett's Folk and Blues shop. Thanks also to Beverly Cox for the loan of her typewriter and to Sonja Kiessling for translations. A special thankyou goes to Pat Bates, without whom none of this would have been possible.

Prerap

Rapping is a word that has been a part of Afro-American vocabulary for a long time. With the coming of a new black American popular music called Rap in 1979, people all over the world began to be aware of it – thinking of it as a description of rhythmic talking over a funk beat. The first so-called rap records were in fact the tip of an iceberg – under the surface was a movement called hip hop, a Bronx-based subculture, and beneath that was a vast expanse of sources reaching back to West Africa. The praise singing, social satires and boasting of savannah Griots that appeared to reincarnate in groups with names like Grandmaster Flash and The Furious Five, Afrika Bambaataa and Cosmic Force, The Treacherous Three and The Funky Four Plus One More, had all been present in black music over the last 80 years. Where once they were relegated to the sidelines of language studies, the service industries of music like radio, or aspects of blues and soul lyricism, they were now centre stage and in the charts.

For listeners who aren't diehard fans, rap tends to be the same as blues, reggae or jazz – it's 'boring', it's 'repetitive'. The pop cover versions are more 'intelligent'. It's also seen as a self-contained phenomenon which will probably go away before too long. How self-contained is a record like 'Ya Mama' by a group called Wuf Ticket? A pretty average release, musically speaking, it was a direct reference to black street slang and word battles like the dozens, signifying, gaming and woofing. As such, it connected back to blues, R&B and soul releases from earlier periods like Speckled Red's 'The Dirty Dozens', Luther Ingram's 'Puttin' Game Down' and Bo Diddley's 'Say Man' – even rap poetry/music like Melvin Van Peebles's 'The Dozens' or comedy routines like Richard Pryor's 'I Spy Cops'.

Although it is impossible to interconnect all the different strands and influences which have contributed to the development of hip hop and do justice to all of them, I have tried to convey the depth of tradition that has led to records like 'Planet Rock', 'The Message', 'The Crown' and the many other leaders of the Rap Attack. Each chapter deserves its own book and I hope will one day get it.

TIMES SQUARE BOX

PEDRO
COLON

STUDS AND GLOVES AT DANCETERIA

DRUGS
LIVE

1. On the corner

Ten thirty p.m. on a cold Saturday night in January and three b boys are working their pitch near Times Square, New York City. The spectators have just paid to watch Clint Eastwood blow away a selection of black stick-up men and multi-cultural rapists. They settle down to a few free moments with uptown culture.

Eddie is 10 years old. He has been break-dancing and moonwalking on the streets around this block since he was 6, using a strip of cardboard as a dancefloor. The two others in the crew are 16, one of them huddled in a sheepskin, the other with the top of his head pushed into a stocking. Both of them pat the beat for Eddie with hand-claps, taking turns to rap. Whether I believe their claims that they appeared in Charlie Ahearn's hip-hop movie *Wildstyle* is neither here nor there; the most important thing they want to put across to me is that they know everybody on the block.

On West 52nd and 10th Avenue Daniel Ponce has just finished his first set at Soundscape. The standout number for me is an interpretation of a Beny Moré bolero, played with great sensitivity and facility by saxophonist Paquito D'Rivera. Ponce is a Cuban with a rep as a great bata and conga player. Though his live shows combine Cuban folklore with jazz he is also becoming known for adding the Latin ingredient to beat-box tracks fronted by Herbie Hancock, Material and Grandmixer D.ST – recordings which combine the innovations of scratch mixing and turntable cutting with the most advanced percussion and keyboard technology.

The two extremes of hip hop are the sophisticated cross-cultural fusions which meld the oldest traditions with the freshest of musical technologies or, at the other pole and clinging for life, the bottom line of street survival. They are indicative of the sharp contrasts within its city of origin, New York. Hip hop's home, The Bronx, is an area with a fearsome reputation caricatured by films such as *Bronx Warriors* and *Fort Apache: The Bronx*. Its grim project housing and burnt-out buildings have little of the political and cultural resonance of neighbouring Harlem, let alone the material assets further downtown; it was within The Bronx and, to a lesser extent, Harlem that black youths developed their own alternative to the gang warfare that had risen from the dead in the late 1960s to dominate and divide neighbourhoods north of Central Park.

It was a DJ style which helped to create the lifestyle which came to be known as hip hop. At the beginning of the disco era in the first half of the 1970s, regular disco jocks in clubs were most concerned with the blend between one record and the next – matching tempos to make a smooth transition which, at its best, could continually alter the mood on the dancefloor without breaking the flow. At its worst the technique could turn the night into one endless and inevitably boring song.

FRESH BREAKERS AT THE ROXY

KICKS

In The Bronx, however, the important part of the record was the break – the part of a tune in which the drums take over. It could be the explosive Tito Puente style of Latin timbales to be heard on Jimmy Castor records; the loose funk drumming of countless '60s soul records by legends like James Brown or Dyke and The Blazers; even the foursquare bass-drum-and-snare intros adored by heavy metal and hard rockers like Thin Lizzy and The Rolling Stones. That was when the dancers flew and DJs began cutting between the same few bars on two turntables, extending the break into an instrumental. One copy of a record – forget it.

The dances featuring these off-the-wall mobile jocks, at first held in schools, community centres, house parties and parks, helped bring former rival gangs together. In the transition from outright war the hierarchical gang structure mutated into comparatively peaceful groups, called crews. Over a period of five years the crews contributed to the development of hip hop. Since nobody in New York City, America or the rest of the world wanted to know about the black so-called ghettoes – the unmentionable areas of extreme urban deprivation – the style was allowed to flourish as a genuine street movement whose presence was felt only through the prominence of one aspect of the culture – graffiti.

White New Yorkers might never have to visit the black or Hispanic parts of town; in that sense graffiti was a visitation upon them. A relic from a past age of streetcorner men and warrior gangs, graffiti had progressed from a scribbled tag (nickname) or club name on the wall to an elaborate art form emblazoned with Magic Marker and spray paint over every available surface of the subway trains and buildings. If the city refused to come to young blacks and Puerto Ricans, then they would go to the city. The rest of the culture was a private affair – truly underground. The DJs teamed up with MCs who provided a show, creating spoken rhymes, catch phrases and a commentary about the DJ, the clientele and themselves over the beats:

When I was born my momma gave birth
to the baddest MC on the goddam earth

A style of dress grew up – a fractured image of cool, combining casual and sports wear – and the dancing was fiercely competitive. Competition was at the heart of hip hop. Not only did it help displace violence and the refuge of destructive drugs like heroin, but it also fostered an attitude of creating from limited materials. Sneakers became high fashion; original music was created from turntables, a mixer and obscure (highly secret) records; entertainment was provided with the kind of showoff street rap that almost any kid was capable of turning on a rival.

In 1979 the b boys and b girls (as they had come to be known) were in for a shock. From seemingly nowhere, two singles were released to send hip hop public. First Fatback, a waning street funk group from Brooklyn, put out a record on Spring with an unknown disc jockey called King Tim III. It was a rap called 'King Tim III

BOMBING THE 6 TRAIN

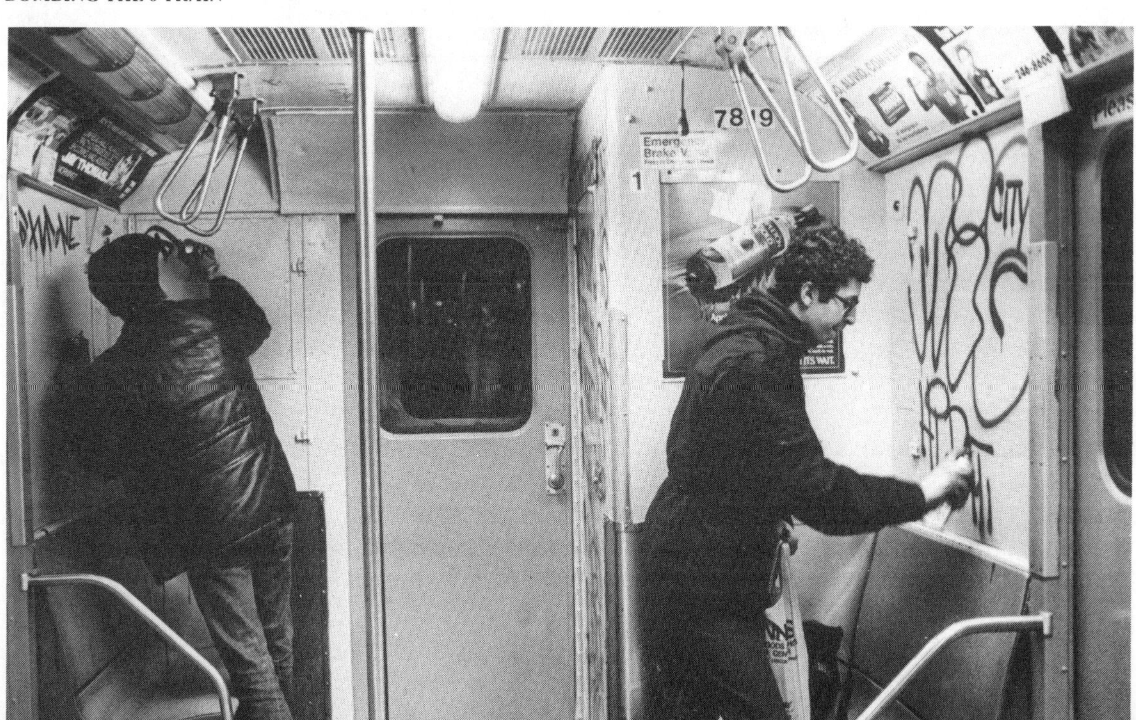

(Personality Jock)'. Second, The Sugarhill Gang, a trio who were also unknowns, had their 'Rapper's Delight' launched on Sugarhill Records. Though Fatback's record was a success of sorts, its style harked back to the days when radio rapping jocks heated up the airwaves with rhyming jive. 'Rapper's Delight', on the other hand, not only stole MC rapping but also appropriated the idea of using a remake of Chic's huge disco hit 'Good Times' as its backing track. The response from the hip-hop community was a contradictory mixture of resentment and a desire to get in on the action.

During the next few years the rush to sign deals was largely accommodated by relatively small-scale, uptown independents whose guiding lights were familiar names from the past three decades of New York black music. At the centre were Enjoy Records and Sugarhill, with a number of smaller labels – Winley, Sound of New York USA, Holiday – popping up with rap records to underline further the fact that this was the Harlem shuffle.

Sylvia Robinson (Sugarhill), Bobby Robinson (Enjoy), Danny Robinson (Holiday) and Paul Winley (Winley) had all been involved in the New York music scene since the 1950s. With the exception of Sylvia, none of these entrepreneurs had ventured far into the increasingly racially integrated disco market. While the rest of the music industry was being saved (and subsequently near-ruined) by their exploitation of disco, the R&B and doo-wop veterans stood by in contempt or bewilderment, unable to identify with beats-per-minute, Studio 54 and all the more blatant high-living trappings imposed on the genre. Rapping, by comparison, bore a striking resemblance to the street-corner harmony era. Just as the 115th Street Tin Can Band had honed their routines in their playground at Wadleigh Junior High (later becoming The Harptones) back in 1951 so, 25 years later, it would have been possible to peer through the wire-mesh fence of a similar schoolyard and hear schoolfriends and neighbours struggling to arrange ensemble raps and solo verses in preparation for a block party.

ADVENTURES ON THE WHEELS OF STEEL: GRANDMASTER FLASH AT BROADWAY INTERNATIONAL

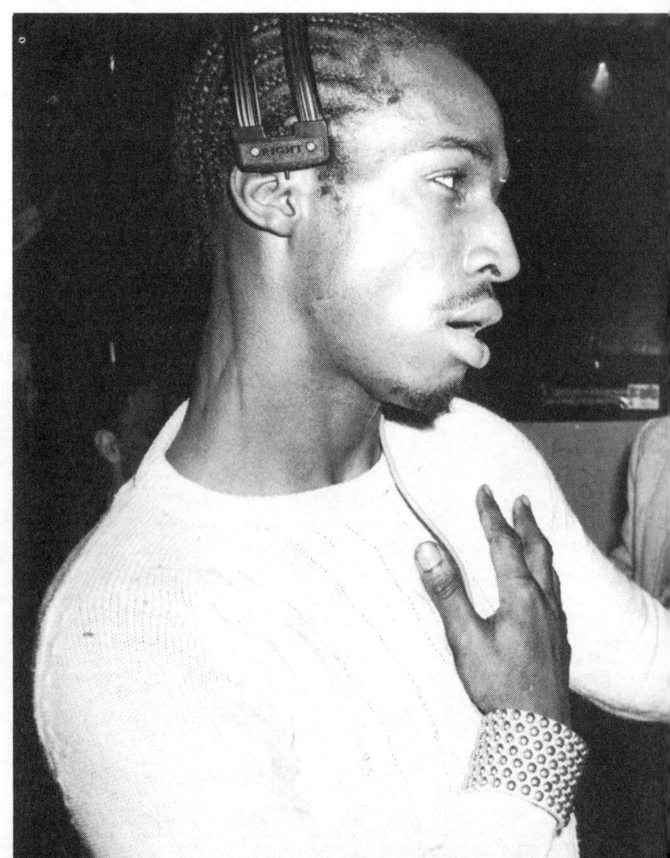

The veterans were now of an age to be able to follow their children. For Sylvia Robinson it was partly the enthusiasm of her son which led her to record The Sugarhill Gang; Paul Winley had his daughter, a 'rap fanatic', to spur him into action, and Bobby Robinson watched his nephew, Spoonie Gee, writing rhymes in the front room of the Robinson apartment. None of these old hands could be attributed with musical genius – their talent had always lain in spotting a certain kind of musical potential. Their record label credits as producer and co-writer might simply indicate their experience in sharpening a tune for the marketplace (if it wasn't just for fronting the money). Both label owners and rappers depended on skilled and versatile musicians who, like Mickey 'Guitar' Baker (a lynchpin of R&B recordings of the '50s), channelled their abilities as jazz musicians into arrangements which were as tough and as calculatedly direct as they were elementary. In the early days of rap on wax, it was musicians like Pumpkin at Enjoy and Jiggs Chase at Sugarhill who defined a new musical style. In its educated simplicity it was as New York as the rent party stride piano of James P. Johnson, the 'jump' band blues of Louis Jordan or the small-group disco of Chic.

Because most rappers started out with a DJ playing records for musical accompaniment (no live musicians), many rap records are based around the chords and bass lines of popular songs. In the early days they were instrumentals – Herbie Hancock or Bob James – and instrumental sections from vocal discs, but as it became standard to put the backing track of the topside song on the B side of 12-inch singles, so it became easier to make a rap over a hit tune. The practice was nothing new – there are plenty of seven-inch singles which do the same thing – but the length of the tracks on a 12-inch (sometimes over 10 minutes) and the width of the grooves, not to mention the fact that there's more *plastic* to get a hold of, made it easier to cut and scratch mix between two copies. To hear Grandmaster Flash cutting up Barbara Mason's story of living with a cross-dressing gay, 'Another Man', at a roots club like Broadway Inter-

BROADWAY INTERNATIONAL 146TH AND BROADWAY

national on 146th Street is an education. Like watching transformation effects in modern horror movies like *The Thing* or *The Howling*, the endless high-speed collageing of musical fragments leaves you breathless, searching for reference points. The beauty of dismembering hits lies in displacing familiarity. It gives the same thrill that visitors to Minton's Playhouse must have felt in the 1940s hearing Charlie Parker carve up standards like 'I Got Rhythm'. Parker wrote many tunes in this way, of course, including 'Ornithology', a bebop standard based on the chords of 'How High The Moon'. When Babs Gonzalez added words (as both Eddie Jefferson and King Pleasure did with 'Parker's Mood' and many other jazz tunes and solos) he was creating one of the many Harlem-based antecedents of rap – jive lyrics superimposed on a dislocated version of a popular tune of the day.

The parallel also applies to reggae toasting, a form of music-making that was strongly influenced by American jive-talking radio disc jockeys and MCs. Although reggae was relatively unknown to most black Americans in the early '70s the links between New York and the Caribbean are strong. In the 1930s almost one-quarter of Harlem's residents were from the West Indies. For Grandmaster Flash, whose parents came from Barbados (his father collected records of both Caribbean music and American swing), it was the 'monstrous' sound system of Kool DJ Herc which dominated hip hop in its formative days. Herc came from Kingston, Jamaica, in 1967, when the toasting or DJ style of his own country was still fairly new. Giant speaker boxes were essential in the competitive world of Jamaican sound systems (sound-system battles were and still are central to the reggae scene) and Herc murdered the Bronx opposition with his volume and shattering frequency range.

Despite charismatic and influential figures like Flash or Zulu Nation leader DJ Afrika Bambaataa being meticulous in giving the lower-profile Herc a share of the limelight, the competitive spirit still flares among b boys (though seemingly less so among the b girls). For Bobby Robinson the contradiction is clear: 'Damn it, every group I meet is number one! Are there no number twos?'

Whatever the disagreements over lineage in the rap hall of fame or the history of hip hop, there is one thing on which all are agreed. 'Rap is nothing new', says Paul Winley. Rap's forebears stretch back through disco, street funk, radio DJs, Bo Diddley, the bebop singers, Cab Calloway, Pigmeat Markham, the tap dancers and comics, The Last Poets, Gil Scott-Heron, Muhammad Ali, acappella and doo-wop groups, ring games, skip-rope rhymes, prison and army songs, toasts, signifying and the dozens, all the way to the griots of Nigeria and the Gambia. No matter how far it penetrates into the twilight maze of Japanese video games and cool European electronics, its roots are still the deepest in all contemporary Afro-American music.

AFRIKA BAMBAATAA

JESSIE LOVE'S BOX

MICHAEL JACKSON
MICHAEL JACKSON
SHARP
eject
pause
GF MUSIC
FM / FM STEREO
RECORDER

2. Doo-wop hip hop

Street culture has always been a good sales pitch for pushing vicarious thrills on the mass market. For a brief pause in all the phoney realism of *Flashdance*, the hyped-up dance movie of 1983, one of the sources for Jennifer Beal's overblown dance routines comes to life. Like a revisitation of Bill 'Bojangles' Robinson teaching Shirley Temple how to tap, the heroine takes in a few seconds of The Rock Steady Crew doing their robot routines in the park to the accompaniment of a huge portable tape box.

The music on the box is a hip-hop anthem – Jimmy Castor's 'It's Just Begun' – a hard dance track from 1972 which fuses one-chord riffing, a Sly Stone pop bridge, fuzz guitar, timbales breaks and an idealistic lyric applicable to any emergent movement, be it dance, music, politics or religion. It gives an impression of the breadth of Jimmy Castor's music and its reflection of the New York mix, encapsulating an involvement which dates back to the beginning of rock 'n' roll.

Hip hop is a peculiarly New York phenomenon in the same way that Jimmy Castor is a specifically New York musician. Born in 1943, he was an understudy for Frankie Lymon with The Teenagers by the age of 14, later developing an infectious dance music with a constant ear to the street and a capacity to absorb and introduce other influences. Early tracks like 'Block Party' are a link between the rent parties of the 1920s – functions at which Harlem stride pianists like Fats Waller, Willie the Lion Smith and James P. Johnson contested their skills – and the house parties and outdoor park gatherings which were the scene of hip-hop sound-system and rapping battles in the '70s. The break in 'Block Party' is a surprising eight-bar injection of Latin rhythm into the frantic 4/4 beat of the rest of the tune, a reminder that Jimmy was in the centre of the Latin Soul movement of the middle '60s. Other releases from the same period move from doo-wop and pop through to Motown-style stompers and

THE EVERYTHING MAN: JIMMY CASTOR

saxophone-guitar instrumentals with a pronounced white feel.

With songs like 'Hey Leroy, Your Mama's Callin' ' and later 'Say Leroy (The Creature From the Black Lagoon Is Your Father)', he introduced the insult contests known as the dozens as a dancefloor gimmick and threw yet another line back in time to the beginnings of Afro-American oral traditions and forward into the future to the embryonic rap scene.

It is hard to believe that the youthful Jimmy Castor's start in the music business came in an era notorious for its casualty rate, but he explains how a no-nonsense mother and a personal business sense have taken him from the streetcorner music of the '50s to hero status in the streetcorner music of the '70s and '80s:

> Frankie Lymon, Leslie Uggams and myself went to the same elementary school – Public School 169 in Manhattan. It's upper Manhattan, Sugar Hill they call it. Washington Heights it's actually called. It was a primarily white school. It was really Polish and Irish up there then – it's all Spanish now, and black. Whenever there was an assembly or show they always called on us – I was the shyest. Leslie could always sing. I never understood what she was singing because she always sang legitimate songs when we were into doo-wop. Frankie was just a born – a natural – entertainer and I had to learn. I acquired it but I was a musician 'cos when I left that school I was chosen to attend the music classes in junior high school so Frankie went to that school and Mitch Miller picked Leslie up.
>
> Frankie cut a record when he was 13 and I came running round to the grocery store. I said, 'You cut a *record*?' – that was a big thing. He had just cut 'Why Do Fools Fall In Love?' We would hang out together – Frankie was much more mature than I was. Frankie had ladies at the time that were 25 or 26 and he was 13. My mother was very strict – I had to be in at eight so I couldn't hang. I had a group called Jimmy Castor and the Juniors. I was writing a few songs and I wrote a song called 'I Promise To Remember' which Frankie heard and loved and took

it to George Goldner and the rest is history.

With records like 'I Promise To Remember' and 'Why Do Fools Fall In Love?' on Goldner's Gee label, Frankie Lymon and the Teenagers were a huge influence on New York's aspiring young singers. If the money from their success encouraged Frankie into the high living which contributed to his premature death, Jimmy Castor used his composer royalties from 'I Promise To Remember' with some thoughts to the future:

> That took me right out of the ghetto. I said, 'Mom, we're moving'. My first cheque was huge – it was a gold record. I eventually become Frankie's stand-in. Frankie was blossoming into a tremendous star — The Teenagers were the first supergroup. Herman [Santiago] and Jimmy [Merchant] still have the group. Sherman [Garnes] died. In fact we were gonna sit him up in the hospital bed – he wasn't dead – he was that sick – just to take the pictures. Joe Negroni died of a brain haemorrhage, and Frankie died, of course. I was very close with all of them 'cos we were going on the road together. I could only go weekends though – my mother made me stay in school.
>
> I went to music and art high school – that's where I learnt all my arranging but that's as far as it went. I was a stand-in. I wasn't on the same level because he had an ego and he wasn't easy to get along with. When he didn't show I was there. He had a better voice – what he did in natural I did in falsetto. He tapped, then I took tap lessons from Cholly Atkins. Frankie got heavy into drugs – we had to lock him up a lot of times and keep him away from that. Once he got out he could get wasted.
>
> All through that period it was Richard Barrett who started everything. See, when you mention Bobby Robinson, Richard Barrett, Paul Winley – these people are the cornerstones of what we hear today.

Jimmy also sang with Lewis Lymon and the Teenchords, a group led by Frankie Lymon's brother and recorded by Bobby Robinson, and played saxophone with Dave 'Baby' Cortez (of 'Rinky Dink' fame). His own band worked at Paul Winley's Jazzland Ballroom on Harlem's 125th Street, playing tunes like 'Tequila' for social clubs, and later did the 99-cent dances run by Winley and disc jockey Jocko Henderson at the Audubon Ballroom. From watching or hearing records of Latin musicians like Tito Puente, Chano Pozo and Cal Tjader he learned to incorporate authentic Afro-Cuban rhythms and percussion, adding timbales to his vocal and multi-instrumental abilities.

His music is fascinating, partly as a mini history of New York music and partly because of his tendency to recycle his own material in periodic updates. His witty use of jive talk in tracks like 'Dracula' from the 1976 *E Man Groovin'* album makes him a part of the rap music heritage, and in 1983 he recorded his own moralist rap, '(Tellin' On) The Devil', alongside a re-recording of

THE FORCE MDs: TRISCO, MERCURY, TCD AND JESSIE

'It's Just Begun', made in deference to its celebrity status on the hip-hop scene.

'It's Just Begun' is occasionally used by Staten Island group The Force MDs as entrance music for their show. Whatever should happen to this group in the future – fame, oblivion or any other of the limited choices available – their career up until their first record is an uncanny echo of Jimmy Castor's. With an average age of about 20, they are able to combine rapping and breakdancing with formation steps and vocal harmony which draws from doo-wop, acappella, '60s Motown, The Jackson Five, The Persuasions, television theme tunes and commercials. They can create an orchestrated human drum machine with their combined voices and do impressions ranging from Elvis Presley and Michael Jackson to the gravel-voiced Mr T. Like

Jimmy Castor before them, they encapsulate over 30 years of Afro-American music with a style that unconsciously includes elements from many decades further back. TCD, one of the most prolific talkers of the group, traces their saga:

> We started in Staten Island. We were called the LDs at first. This was around 1972 – little kids singing. We were imitating The Jackson Five like all the other groups but we sounded exactly like them. We just sung in the streets – songs to make people happy around the neighbourhood. Any time they wanted to be happy they'd come and knock on our doors and we'd come out singing! We started to do our own thing. One of our brothers became a Muslim. Another one moved away, so it was just us three left. We was working on harmony – getting everything right – going on Broadway and 42nd. So we bumped into Trisco and Mercury. Mercury was like a conjunction with Stevie D, my brother. They used to do a rap thing.

Stevie D and Mercury oblige with a high-powered rap that swaps back and forth between them and ends up with an inspired borrowing of the melody line from 'Santa Claus Is Coming To Town'. TCD continues the story:

> We used to entertain on the Staten Island ferry boat. People liked us a lot. What really got us known was rapping – we rapped in a lot of parts of New York, Jersey and Connecticut. People in Connecticut, when they hear these guys rap they'd make a tape and the tape would travel all the way down south – California, Florida. It just travels everywhere where that person goes. It goes in the army. The guys who used to listen to it recruit into the army and take the tapes with them.

From their classic acappella streetcorner origins The Force MDs expanded their repertoire by working with a DJ named Dr Rock who used all the scratching and cutting techniques developed in the south and west Bronx.

Scratching in its early form arose out of the normal technique of cueing a record: you move the record manually with the needle in the groove and listen for the right starting point on a headphone. One turntable is used for cueing while the other is playing a record through the main loudspeakers. DJs like Grandmaster Flash began experimenting by switching the mixer from the headphones to the speakers for isolated brass-section chords and drum slaps – augmenting the record that was already playing on the other turntable – and then learned how to use a record percussively by quickly moving it back and forth over the same chord or beat.

Both the showiness and gimmicky sound potential of this kind of creative mixing have supplemented The Force MDs' previously self-contained act. Scratching is used as a witty sound effect for the group's adaptation of TV themes from *The Brady Bunch*, *The Addams Family* and *F Troop*; it also extends into acrobatics and sleight-of-

THE FORCE MDs: TCD AND STEVIE D

hand trickery, as Mercury explains:

> He can cut up with his elbows, his chin, his feet, with handcuffs on, blindfolded. He can make beats with just one turn table. He's a mastermind on turntables. He can put the turntables on the floor and scratch with his feet . . . We have a back-up DJ. His name is Dr Shock – this guy, he goes crazy when it comes to scratching. He can take a record and put a cup underneath it – play the record backwards with the needle upside down and make scratching. He can scratch a record till it has a hole in it.

Much to the rest of the group's amusement, Mercury can reproduce most of Rock and Shock's sounds with his mouth; if the electricity gives out, then this group, along with many others like it, has the pedigree to carry on and hold the clientele.

In 1947, when the American folk-music collector Alan Lomax took a portable tape recorder (the first to appear on the market) into the horrific conditions of the Mississippi State Penitentiary, he recorded black acappella vocal music, which he claimed demonstrated 'that true African polyphony and poly-rhythm have somehow survived in the Southern US until our own epoch' (sleevenotes to *Negro Prison Songs*, Tradition Records reissue LP TLP 1020). The city can be a prison, too, and in many ways the formative neighbourhood vocalising of The Force MDs is part of a continuum that reaches back not just to the days when a 13-year-old Jimmy Castor was singing in school (hoping to make enough money to escape the ghetto) but even further to the group vocalising that made forced labour more bearable in prisons and plantations.

If the association seems far fetched, it's partly because the imagery has changed so dramatically – the mythological tricksters and heroes are replaced by electronic-age superheroes recruited from kung fu, karate, science fiction and blaxploitation movies, re-run television series, video games, comic books and advertising. The central heroes, of course, are the rappers themselves, aggressively claiming respect (as a means of finding self respect) with the same expertise in verbal improvisation as that wielded by streetcorner orators, stand-up comics, testifying preachers and vernacular poets for generations.

3. African jive

I float like a butterfly, sting like a bee,
There ain't no motherfucker than can rap
like me

'CC Crew Rap' by CC Crew
(Golden Flamingo Records)

In 1964 the white world was finding it hard to understand a young black boxer named Cassius Clay. Bill McDonald, the promoter of his first crack at Sonny Liston's world heavyweight title, and trainer Angelo Dundee, were failing to appreciate his reasons for associating with Elijah Muhammad and Malcolm X. The Nation of Islam was bad news in the white-run fight game. Those less close to the Clay camp were mystified by his seemingly hysterical behaviour and his rap poetry, the infuriating rhymes which predicted the demise of his opponents: 'Sonny Liston is great/But he'll fall in eight.'

The unfortunate Liston had a better idea of what was going on. An ex-badman, he was well aware that Clay (at the time secretly known as Cassius X but later known to the world as Muhammad Ali), along with his personal shaman, Drew Bundini Fastblack Brown, was engaged in a campaign to shame him into defeat before the first bell. Ali was prepared to take the campaign to Liston's home and remind his well-heeled white neighbours of their new resident's background in the black ghetto. History records that Liston was humiliated twice by Ali. Fight fans with a white complexion would have been less puzzled by the young braggard whipping the awesome monster if they had known something of black street culture.

The Clay versus Liston scenario has a storyline reminiscent of the famous black narrative poem called 'Signifying Monkey'. The monkey is a trickster who taunts the lion, despite its size and strength, and outwits it with verbal skill:

There hadn't been no shift for quite a bit
so the Monkey thought he'd start some of
his signifying shit.
It was one bright summer day
the Monkey told the Lion, 'There's a big
bad burly motherfucker livin' down
your way.'
He said, 'You know your mother that you
love so dear?
Said anybody can have her for a ten-cent
glass a beer.'

These kind of narrative poems are called toasts. They are rhyming stories, often lengthy, which are told mostly amongst men. Violent, scatalogical, obscene, misogynist, they have been used for decades to while away time in situations of enforced boredom, whether prison, armed service or streetcorner life. Bruce Jackson, who has made extensive studies of toasts and prison songs, has written:

> There is much time to kill in county jails and little to do with that time, and a great portion of the population in county jails is lower-class black (they are the people

without money to pay a bondsman for freedom before trial or who must serve jail time because they lack money to pay a fine).

Toasts, like most oral folk traditions, have become absorbed into commercial entertainment, albeit in a censored form. 'Stackolee', a badman figure familiar from many blues and ballads performed by both black and white musicians, was resurrected by Lloyd Price in 1958 as 'Stagger Lee' for a chart-topping hit and was revived for another shoot-out by The Isley Brothers in 1963. A year later, Rufus Thomas, a remarkable man whose career stretched right back to the medicine-show era, released a tune called 'Jump Back' on Stax. Though the sound is typical of the bluesy soul of the time – uptempo and rough, with cutting saxophone and guitar breaks – the verses of the song date back at least as far as nineteenth-century minstrel shows; a children's line-game song, 'Mary Mack' quoted by Harold Courlander in his book *Negro Folk Music*, has almost identical words:

I went to the river, river, river,
And I couldn't get across, across, across,
And I paid five dollars, dollars, dollars,
For the old grey horse, horse, horse.

JUMP BACK: RUFUS THOMAS *Photo: courtesy of Charlie Gillett*

Thomas used another verse from 'Mary Mack' for his 'Walking the Dog', another revival, this time of a dance that was around in the early 1900s. Although parts of 'Jump Back' had also been collected as a work-song, they were first made famous by Thomas Rice, a white dancer who performed blackface and whose stage name was Daddy 'Jim Crow' Rice. The legend goes that Rice had the good fortune to see a black slave named after his owner, Jim Crow, doing a song and dance with a great potential for the stage. Rice stole the idea, added some verses and by the end of the 1820s had a craze going for himself, not only through America but also as far away as England and Ireland.

Rufus Thomas's reappropriation of 'Jump Jim Crow' was poetic justice. Working as a tapdancer, scat singer and all-round entertainer with the Rabbit Foot Minstrels in the 1930s, he felt the effects of racism both on and off stage.

For 'Jody's Got Your Girl and Gone', Johnny Taylor (a singer who, like Rufus Thomas, recorded for Stax) revived Jody, a character also known in toasts as Joe the Grinder. Jody's exploits, sung or narrated in prison or the army, symbolised the fear that somebody might be stealing your lover back home. Although the spoken toast fell into decline, the song version of the story – often about G.I. Joe returning from the war and finding Jody in bed with his wife – was still being sung in army camps in the 1970s, and Johnny Taylor's reworking is a testament to the longevity of the story's potency.

The cross talk between popular entertainment drawn back into folklore and mists-of-time traditions facelifted for contemporary styles can make it impossible to pinpoint origins. A toast collected by Bruce Jackson on Wynne Prison Farm in Texas in 1966 – 'Ups On the Farm' – and said by Jackson to be 'the only toast I've heard that expressly deals with black/white problems' was, in fact, part of Butterbeans and Susie's repertoire. Butterbeans and Susie were a husband and wife comedy singing/dancing act whose recordings spanned 40 years, from 1922 to 1962, and they formed part of a venerable tradition of comedy teams whose popularity was established on the TOBA (Theater Owner's Booking Association) black vaudeville circuit. A later team, Moke and Poke, were said by Marshall and Jean Stearns in *Jazz Dance* to 'conduct their dialogue in hip rhymes. "We're Moke and Poke, it ain't no joke, that's all she wrote, the pencil broke." '

Jazz Dance also notes the way in which the comedy dance teams developed a razor-sharp satirical humour aimed at and for black audiences, making the point that:

> One of its sources was probably the West African song of allusion (where the subject pays the singer *not* to sing about him), reinterpreted in the West Indies as the political calypso, in New Orleans as the 'signifying' song, and in the South generally as 'the dozens'.

Although at least some of the origins of this rich material could be traced to the Bible or British folk songs, it had clear roots in West Africa. Ruth Finnegan, in her book *Oral Literature in Africa*, describes how poetry and music could function as a social weapon:

> Lampoons are not only used between groups but can also be a means of communicating and expressing personal enmity between hostile individuals. We hear of Galla abusive poems, for instance, while among the Yoruba when two women have quarrelled they sometimes vent their enmity by singing at each other, especially in situations – like the laundry place – when other women will hear. Abusive songs against ordinary individuals are also sometimes directly used as a means of social pressure, enforcing the will of public opinion.

In the savannah belt of West Africa this social pressure is embodied by the caste of musicians known as griots. The griot is a professional singer, in the past often associated with a village but now an increasingly independent 'gun for hire', who combines the functions of living history book and newspaper with vocal and instrumental virtuosity. According to Paul Oliver in his book *Savannah Syncopators*,

> though he has to know many traditional songs without error, he must also have the ability to extemporise on current events, chance incidents and the passing scene. His wit can be devastating and his knowledge of local history formidable.

Although they are popularly known as praise singers, griots might combine appreciation of a rich employer with gossip and satire or turn their vocal expertise into an attack on the politically powerful or the financially stingy.

If the hip-hop message and protest rappers had an ancestry in the savannah griots, the Bronx braggers, boasters and verbal abusers are children of the black American word games known as signifying and the dozens. During the late 1950s and early '60s a folklore student named Roger D. Abrahams collected tape recordings of many toasts, jokes and verbal contests in the predominantly black area of Camingerly, Philadelphia, where he lived. In his book *Deep Down In the Jungle* he explains the importance of 'good talkers' in Afro-American society, and concentrates particularly on the crucial role of talking skills in male society:

> Verbal contest accounts for a large portion of the talk between members of this group. Proverbs, turns of phrases, jokes, almost any manner of discourse is used, not for purposes of discursive communication but as weapons in verbal battle. Any gathering of the men customarily turns into 'sounding', a teasing or boasting session.

Abrahams found this kind of teasing among children who used 'catches' to trick each other:

> *Say 'washing machine'.*
> *'Washing machine.'*

DESERT GRIOTS FROM SOKOTO, NORTHERN NIGERIA *Photo: Jeremy Marre*

DISCO FEVER

I'll bet you five dollars your drawers ain't clean.

As the participants got older so the contests got more serious – sounding or the dozens could lead to serious fights among adults. The dozens contests were generally between boys and men from the ages of 16 to 26 – a semi-ritualised battle of words which batted insults back and forth between the players until one or the other found the going too heavy. The insults could be a direct personal attack but were more frequently aimed at the opponent's family and in particular his mother. According to linguist William Labov, who studied these verbal shoot-outs in Harlem in the 1960s, 'In New York, "the dozens" seems to be even more specialised, referring to rhymed couplets of the form:

I don't play the dozens, the dozens ain't my game
But the way I fucked your mama is a god damn shame.'

Working with teenage clubs like the Jets and the Cobras, Labov came across poetic insults like, 'Your mother play dice with the midnight mice', and more elaborate exchanges which are like fully developed comedy routines:

Boot: Hey! I went up Money house and I walked in Money house, I say, I wanted to sit down, and then, you know a roach jumped up and said, 'Sorry, this seat is taken.'
Roger: I went in David house, I saw the roaches walking round in combat boots.

The distance between talking rough with the dozens on the streets and moving it inside a roots club like Disco Fever with some beats for dancing is very small. It leads to the contradictions of Melle Mel, lyricist for the Furious Five, onstage in his ultra-macho metal warrior outfit trying to preach convincingly for an end to machismo and a beginning to peaceful co-existence.

Out among the grown-ups the dozens

TIMES SQUARE CLIFFHANGER

thrive in the 'dirty party' genre with a host of little-known comedians. You can also find Johnny Otis with Snatch and the Poontangs, the very funny Redd Foxx, the very unfunny Rudy Ray Moore whose record covers scale the greatest heights of porno-kitsch, and the notorious Blowfly. Blowfly, the unacceptable face of rap, is the pseudonym of Miami singer/producer Clarence Reid (the man who co-wrote 'Clean Up Woman' with Little Beaver for Betty Wright and released it on the Alston label).

One of the clearest links between present-day rappers and the rich vein of tall tales, tricksters, boasts and insults is Bo Diddley. Describing the type of rapping he was doing when he started out, Mr Biggs of Soul Sonic Force recollects that, 'we used to call it a Bo Diddley syndrome when we used to brag amongst ourselves'. Bo is the bragger *par excellence* – his street-talk boasts were originally combined with a unique Afro-Latin sound of maraccas, floor tom toms played by drummer Frank Kirkland and his own customised and distinctly weird guitar. His first single, recorded in 1955 for Chess Records in Chicago, was a double-sided punch on the nose for modesty – on the A side the ultimate macho anthem 'I'm a Man' and on the B side Diddley's personal plaudit called, aptly enough, 'Bo Diddley'.

Many of his later songs used material from toasts and the dozens: 'Who Do You Love', the story of a satanic badman who wears a cobra snake for a necktie, is like a toast in itself, using lines almost identical to Stackolee's 'I'm a bad motherfucker, that's why I don't mind dying'. Other songs use familiar themes – 'The Story of Bo Diddley' with its full-grown baby playing a gold guitar, 'Run Diddley Daddy' and its rumble-in-the-jungle tall tale and 'Say Man', a record which grew out of Bo and maracca player Jerome trading the dozens in the studio. Put down on tape with some judicious editing, it became one of Bo's biggest hits, striking back at the record company notion that too much black content keeps records out of the charts.

'Say Man' is the great-grandfather of the rap attack. The anonymous Ronnie Gee prepares the crowd for his 'Raptivity', a tall tale of microphone battles that run deep in the night leaving heart attacks in their wake: 'Warning – the surgeon general of chilltown New York has determined that the sounds you are about to hear can be devastating to your ear-ear-ear-ear-ear.'

SAY MAN: BO DIDDLEY, THE DUCHESS, AND JEROME
Photo: courtesy of Charlie Gillett

4. Beat bop

On a summer afternoon in 1979 at Columbia University in the middle of Harlem, Milford Graves is on stage drumming with his long-term associate, saxophonist Hugh Glover, and Japanese trumpeter Toshinori Kondo. The event is the Third Annual Children of the Sun concert with Baba Chief Bey, the Afrikan Poetry Theatre Ensemble and other guests. Strictly speaking, Milford is not on the stage; for a time he moves out into the audience with two long poles, speaking in strange tongues before getting back on the platform to launch into another whirlwind drum dialogue with Glover. His vocalising, an astonishing flow of percussive syllables, could be seen as one of the furthest outposts of the scat tradition – represented at the other pole by great jazz singers like Louis Armstrong, Ella Fitzgerald and Betty Carter.

For singers like these (including Milford Graves) scat is a way of using the voice as a pure instrument, but there is another tradition of scatting which, like rap, took street slang and transformed it into a musical style. Cabell 'Cab' Calloway is one of the cornerstones of jive scat, the author of a number of books including *The New Cab Calloway's Hepster's Dictionary*, and a bandleader in New York from 1930 to 1948. Cab appears in *Stormy Weather* (the 1943 equivalent of *Wildstyle* or *Beat Street*), a film loosely constructed around the great tapdancer Bill 'Bojangles' Robinson. Alongside Robinson was an all black cast – Lena Horne, Fats Waller, one of the original New York rappers with his hilarious jive disruptions of songs, and a host of eccentric dancers (rubber face antics), flash dancers and tapdancers. In the middle of this firework display of '40s black talent Cab Calloway is still a shock. Resplendent in a capacious zoot suit with chain and long greased hair, he glides across the stage in a move that pre-dates moonwalking by 40 years.

Cab was one of the out-front bandleaders, a conductor who sang, danced and provided a focal point for the audience. Working at the famous Cotton Club on 142nd and Lennox Avenue, the nightspot where rich whites came to indulge their fantasies about the noble savage, Calloway mixed up call-and-response scatting (on 'Zah Zuh Zah' Cab sings variants on the title and the audience and orchestra repeat whatever new outrage he comes up with), jive lyrics with coded references to drugs ('Kicking the Gong Around' or 'Viper's Drag'), or chat and scat talkovers like 'Harlem Camp Meeting' with the immortal lines, 'That's it, son, your credit for this sermon I'm gonna give you here. Look out now – skipndigipipndibobopakoodoot', as the clarinet player finishes his solo.

This type of commentary could work both ways. There was also a strong tradition of the instrumentalists trying to discourage the singer with half-concealed sarcasm sent out at just enough volume to cross the footlights. Bandleaders like Cab Calloway occupied a role somewhere between the piano-playing leaders like Duke Ellington and Count Basie and the masters of ceremonies who used jive talk and rhyming couplets to introduce the acts – one of the strongest links with hip hop, which started out with rappers talking on the microphone about the skill of the disc jockey. MCs developed their own line of patter to keep a show rolling. Ernie 'Bubbles' Whitman, also known as 'the stomach that walked like a man', was an MC who worked for Billy Eckstine. He was given to flights of fancy on the lines of:

> Yessirree, send me that ballad from Dallas. I'm floating on a swoonbeam. And now to keep the downbeat bouncing right along, here's a zootful snootful called 'Mr Chips', as it is fleeced and released by Billy Eckstine and his trilly tune-tossers. Toss it, Billy, toss it!

Another man with a sharp line in introductions was Slim Gaillard who could be heard from the late 1930s right up until the present prefacing songs with lead-ins in the fashion of: 'We'd like to get together and play a little special arrangement on this new opus, a little number titled "Minuet oh vouty laho reetie o dingo reenie mo in oh vouty sow routie mo oh scoodly reenie mo".' Slim began as a tapdancing guitarist and progressed from that semi-impossibility to playing piano with the backs of his hands and reinterpreting standards with a language and logic all his own. The language was called vout and it made Gaillard into one of the key figures of 1940s jive hipsterism. His musical style would cause Afrika Bambaataa to double take – the easy-going bebop with its fractured vout lyrics could be quick-cut at the drop of a bagel into a few bars of Latin with some Spanish commercials or a sudden skid on the tempo for a dash of Billy Eckstine. The high priest of vout can be seen in the 1942 movie *Hellzapoppin* playing accompaniment for the wildest breakdancing ever seen on film. Slim, along with other hepcats like Harry 'The Hipster' Gibson and Leo Watson, was turning language inside out on the fringes of bebop.

Eddie Jefferson was probably the first of the bebop-era jazz singers to take jazz solos or tunes like Coleman Hawkins's 'Body and Soul' and turn them into vocal improvisations. Jefferson was inspired by the apparently bottomless well of source material in jazz dance and evolved his style by singing over records in the late '30s. His versions of Charlie Parker tunes like 'Parker's Mood' were languid excursions into hip phrasing and phraseology, following up lines of more pauses than words with triple-time tongue-twisters. Jefferson's initiative was taken up by a singer named Clarence Beeks, better known as King Pleasure. Pleasure's vocalmentals versioned jazz solos, taking all the slurs, smears and surges of saxophonists Charlie Parker and Lester Young with their tunes 'Jumping With Symphony Sid' or 'Parker's Mood'.

Another Parker tune, 'Ornithology', based on the chords of 'How High the Moon', was the starting-off point for two of the hippest of hepster anthems – the great

Babs Gonzalez's 'Ornithology' and 'Sugar Ray' (a song about one of the most popular black boxers of all time – Sugar Ray Robinson). Babs was among the cleverest at fitting strings of words around the convoluted Parker melodies while still sounding cool.

In his autobiography *To Be Or Not To Bop*, Dizzy Gillespie writes:

> We added some colorful and creative concepts to the English language, but I can't think of any word besides bebop that I actually invented. Daddy-O Daylie, a disc jockey in Chicago, originated much more of the hip language during our era than I did.

Daddy-O Daylie was one of a number of black radio DJs who from the 1940s until the 1960s lit up the airwaves of America with their hepcat jive – bringing back the live feel to recorded music. One of the first black radio jocks, Dr Hep Cat, shook up listeners to KVET in Austin, Texas, with his crazy couplets:

> *If you want to hip to the tip and bop to the top*
> *You get some mad threads that just won't stop*

Dr Hep Cat's real name was Lavada Durst. He also played piano and sang – recording songs such as 'Hepcat's Boogie' – and in 1953 he published his own hepcat's dictionary, *The Jives of Dr Hep Cat*. In New Orleans, the first black disc jockey was Vernon Winslow, known as Dr Daddy-O, broadcasting for WWEZ in 1949 with his show 'Jivin' with Jax'. Dr Daddy-O's story is a case history in racism. Refused a broadcasting job because of his colour, he was offered the task of training a white announcer to talk black. Winslow organised the whole show for WJMR, writing the script, choosing the records, teaching the DJ how to talk and even selecting a name for him – Poppa Stoppa. In an interview in *Wavelength* magazine, he talks about the origin of the name.

> Poppa Stoppa came out of that rhyme-rap that the people in the street were using. That's what the ghetto produced. The people were trying to mystify outsiders. It became a unique identity and they were proud of it. So I began writing my script in that language. 'Look at your gold tooth in a telephone booth, Ruth – wham bam, thank you, man.' I had a penchant for alliteration.

Eventually, with the 'Jam, Jive and Gumbo' show becoming the most popular shown on WJMR, Winslow grabbed the opportunity to read his own script over the air. He was fired immediately. Six months later he was offered a job by the Jackson Brewing Company as a disc jockey and advertising consultant for Jax beer. Recording his shows in Cosimo Matassa's studio to avoid having to ride the freight elevator at the New Orleans Hotel where the shows were broadcast (another of the destructive humiliations of racism at the time), his show created havoc in radio. Soon everybody had their own jive-talking jock, each with an imitative name like Jack the Cat, Okey

Dokey, Momma Stoppa and Ernie the Whip.

Dr Daddy-O started by playing jazz but was soon playing the new R&B sound of Professor Longhair and Roy Brown. With the coming of hard rhythm and blues and rock 'n' roll, the jiving jocks found a new power: machine-gun poets like Georgie Woods (the guy with the goods), Maurice 'Hotrod' Hulbert from Baltimore, Sonny Hopson on WDAS, Clarence Heyman who took over the Poppa Stoppa title in New Orleans, Dr Jive (Tommy Smalls) and one of the best-known of them all – Douglas 'Jocko' Henderson, the ace from space with his '1280 Rocket' show. Roger Abrahams quotes one of his raps in *Deep Down in the Jungle:*

Be, bebop
This is your Jock
Back on the scene
With a record machine
Saying 'Hoo-popsie-doo,
How do you do?'
When you up, you up,
And when you down, you down,
And when you mess with Jock
You upside down

One of Jocko's favourite expressions was 'great gugga mugga shooga booga', a catchy phrase familiar to collectors of Jamaican ska records. 'The Great Wuga Wuga' by Sir Lord Comic is a fine example of the way in which radio jive was adapted for Jamaican sound-system music. On collecting trips to the States, searching out R&B records for his sound systems back home, Jamaican producer Coxsone Dodd was impressed enough with radio DJs like Jocko to encourage his own top DJ, Count Machouki, to try out the same techniques. In the hothouse competition of the sound systems the idea was rapidly picked up by rivals, eventually to appear on records like Sir Lord Comic's 'Ska-ing West' from 1965: 'Come on you cats, get hep, we're going west'. Machouki and Sir Lord Comic, along with U Roy who recorded a DJ record called 'Your Ace From Space', King Stitt and other lesser-known DJs, developed the Jamaican style of toasting – at first in a similar fashion to the American radio DJs but rapidly transforming it into the form taken on by toasters like Big Youth and Dennis Alcapone through to Eek A Mouse and Yellowman. With his MC crew the Herculoids, the Jamaican-born hip-hop break mixer Kool DJ Herc started a movement which recycled the creativity of black American jive jocks back into the USA – a circle which closed with the recording studio collaboration of Yellowman with Afrika Bambaataa.

Although DJs like Jocko and Dr Jive had many white listeners and imitators (it was white jive jocks like Alan Freed who were crucial in crossing black R&B and doo-wop over to a white audience, and another self-confessed imitator of the black DJ style, Wolfman Jack, is still going strong with his syndicated shows), it was in the black community that their position was strongest. Jocko, Dr Jive and Rocky G began headlining the rhythm and blues shows at The Apollo Theatre (Jocko was first introduced to Apollo owner Bobby Schiffman by

THE APOLLO THEATRE, 125TH STREET

Bobby Robinson) along with jocks like Frankie Crocker and Eddie O'Jay, the man who gave The O'Jays their name. At other times it was the comedians who were required to introduce the shows.

'The first person I really heard do it was Pigmeat Markham. That was the first rap record I ever heard – on a record my father had.' A surprising statement from someone as young as The Fearless Four's Mike C, considering that Pigmeat introduced the routine that Mike is talking about, 'Heah Come De Judge', to the Alhambra Theatre in New York in 1929. He was still turning up new angles on the 'Judge' routine in the '60s, with hip soul versions on Chess Records like 'Sock It To 'Em Judge' (by then aged around 60) and, as the Mighty Mike C says, they are rap records before rap records existed.

Jackie 'Moms' Mabley with her folksy monologues, Timmie 'Clark Dark' Rogers (the man who made a stand against blackface for black comedians), Scoey Mitchlll, Flip Wilson, Nipsey Russell, the very hip Redd Foxx, Richard Pryor and latterly Eddie Murphy are a small selection of the black comedians whose routines are part of the background to rap. In an extraordinary forerunner of the message rap of the 1980s, Ray Scott recorded a mock sermon monologue set to music which was based on a Redd Foxx routine – probably one of the most vitriolic diatribes ever put on a disc. Called 'The Prayer', it was a savagely, lovingly detailed wish-fulfilment fantasy about all the gruesome deaths that might befall the racist governor George Wallace. After Wallace's death, Scott hopes that 14 possums suffering from hydrophobia will break into his casket and eat enough of him to make him look like a gorilla sucking hot Chinese mustard. If all that isn't enough, then the worst fate would be to wake up black.

It was like a political version of the finely detailed voodoo madness of another performer who worked a thin line between comedy and deadly serious rhythm and blues – Screamin' Jay Hawkins. A crazed monologue like 'Alligator Wine' could still give the hip hoppers a run for their money.

Screamin' Jay Hawkins was at the apex of the kind of music that struck terror into the hearts of white American parents in the 1950s – the idea of their children pressing

YOU CAUGHT ME SMILING: SLY STONE

pink ears to the loudspeaker of a radio that was blasting out this blatantly sexual and demonic delirium was too much to bear. The federal payola investigations of 1959–60 helped put paid to it all. One of the job opportunities for ex-radio jocks in the '60s was dance instruction discs – another of the sources of rap's 'throw your hands in the air' formulae. Radio DJs were expert in telling people what to do, so the dance instruction genre came easily to them. Rodney Jones had 'R&B Time' ('hit it to the left – back to the right'); Rufus Thomas, who was a DJ on WDIA in Memphis, was the doyen of dance crazies with his Dogs, Penguins, Robots and Chickens; Sly Stone worked as a DJ on San Francisco radio as well as producing and writing dance discs for Bobby Freeman ('C'mon and Swim'), and Frankie Crocker, whose chequered career rejoiced under names like 'Loveman', 'Black Satin' and 'Hollywood', took a credit on Turbo Records's dance tune 'Ton of Dynamite' – a slight reworking of Willie and the Mighty Magnificents' 'Funky 8 Corners', originally released on All Platinum. After being indicted on payola charges in 1976, Crocker used his enforced sabbatical from New York radio to produce records like 'Love In C Minor' for Casablanca Records. Strictly speaking, they weren't dance instruction discs (more Barry White groaners) but they were hardcore disco records (and absolutely unlistenable now).

Plenty of far superior funk and disco records kept alive a tradition of street slang, radio jive and dance calling with party vocals, dancefloor chants and talkovers – 'Black Water Gold (Pearl)' by African Music Machine, 'Jungle Fever' by Chaka-chas, 'Get On Down' by East Harlem Bus Stop, 'Fruitman' and 'Spirit of the Boogie' by Kool and the Gang, 'Mango Meat' and 'Ali Bom-Ba-Ye' by Mandrill (the rope-a-dope song), 'Do It 'Til You're Satisifed' by B.T. Express, 'O-Wa' by Babatunde Olatunji, 'Rap On Mr D.J.' by Hamilton Bohannon, 'Ali Shuffle' by Alvin Cash and literally hundreds more from the JBs, The Meters, The Ohio Players, War, Fatback, the George Clinton funk empire and Bootsy's Rubber Band all the way to the present with Washington Go-Go groups like Chuck Brown and the Soul Searchers and Trouble Funk or the New York hip hop meets electro-Afro funk of Shango.

George Clinton, in particular, connects strongly with the radio jive DJs – tracks like 'Chocolate City', 'P. Funk (Wants to get funked up)', 'You Shouldn't-Nuf Bit Fish', 'Atomic Dog', 'Loopzilla' and 'Mr Wiggles' are all inspired by radio jocks; 'Mr Wiggles' from *Motor Booty Affair* was rapped by Clinton in the guise of an underwater disc jockey called Mr Wiggles the Worm who quotes freely from Jocko Henderson. It was a natural for George to make his own hip-hop rap records, and 'Dog Talk' by K-9 Corps (based on the rhythm of 'Atomic Dog') and 'Nubian Nut' were both funny

GEORGE CLINTON P FUNKS THE RITZ

SEQUENTIAL

and funky, spanning three and a half decades of Afro-American music creativity with the essence of R&B radio, '80s electronics and an update of the cosmic orchestra concept of Sun Ra. The Afro-Saturnian swing of Ra and his Arkestra with its chants of 'sign up for Outer Spaceways Incorporated' is not *so* very far from 'one nation under a groove'. The Jonzun Crew certainly saw the connection when they recorded 'Space Is the Place' (the title of a 1973 Sun Ra album on Blue Thumb) and thanked Mr Ra on the sleeve of their *Lost In Space* LP.

DON'T TOUCH THAT DIAL: CAPTAIN SKY

Also cruising the ether was Captain Sky, an ex-radio jock from Chicago heavily inspired by the P. Funk Nation. The Captain underlined the radio rap connection with his 'Don't Touch That Dial' (a phrase from a thousand and one Clinton songs) and 'Station Brake', a rap broadcast directly from Station WSKY on a day when nothing really happened. Captain Sky was just one of the mothership commanders and space wanderers whose mission lay in taking *Star Trek* to the stage. Beaming down on New York was Captain Rock, the figurehead of a rap project put together by The Fantastic Aleems (who recorded their own mystic disco album on Prelude in 1977 as Prana People) and Dr Jeckyl and Mr Hyde. Captain Rock was obviously able to buy George Clinton albums in deep space because his 'Cosmic Glide' on Nia Records had all the signs of the Mothership Connection.

GARY BYRD AT W.L.I.B.

Station WSKY may not have much happening but on Gary Byrd's phone-in/chat show on WLIB there's plenty going on. When it comes to black culture and politics, there is so much hidden from view or swept under history's carpet that 24-hour chat shows would be a mere scratch on the surface. Gary began his career in the middle '60s at the age of 17, broadcasting on station WUFO in his home town of Buffalo. Fascinated by the raps of Jocko and 'Hotrod' Hulbert, he tried out one of his own, only to be told that he would lose his job if he did it again. Raps were a dirty word by that time in American radio history. Moving to New York, he was the youngest DJ in the city, and by the early '70s he was creating social protest mastermixes from tracks by War and The Temptations combined with sound effects. He also moved into music-making with his group The Gary Byrd Experience (named after The Jimi Hendrix Experience) and made records produced by the everywhere/everything man, Jimmy Castor. His radio rapping experience became useful when he developed a social programme researching literacy and taking presentations into schools in New York and New Jersey:

> We found that the kids were processing information faster than the school system was able to project it. What was actually happening was that the kids were bored because they were so electronically conditioned by radio and television to get their information that when the teacher walked into the classroom the teacher was completely unaware that what they were in fact giving was a performance. At the end of 10 minutes the kids' attention would wane and the teacher would wonder what happened. The 10-minute wane was having been conditioned by television for the commercial interruption.
>
> We were knee deep in heavy-duty disco fever and I was trying to figure out some way to do something to work with the schools to improve reading levels. My not being an 'educator' but more like a motivator I figured that if you could at least motivate kids to be interested enough in reading that's the first step.
>
> What we did was hook up this programme, which I was doing in rap – which is the way I always perform – and we hooked it into recording artists, the people they admired most. The Jacksons and Muhammad Ali, who, most of them, because they see them in highly verbal but usually memorised improvisational circumstances, don't really see anything around them that indicates that there is any need to read anything.
>
> We had shots of all the different artists and I'd do raps and show them inside of the raps what has happening with each individual on the outside of what they saw. So, in other words, you had to understand that Michael Jackson didn't just walk into the studio and start singing the tune! 'So they write those songs?' You get that kind of reaction. 'Oh, so Michael reads it, then he learns it. Oh. Ahh.' A lot of surprise there.

Through his work in schools Gary also found that many American blacks were unaware that the Nile civilisation was a part of black history. His raps had already surfaced to a small extent on Stevie Wonder's 'Black Man' from the *Songs In the Key of Life* album. The last part of the song is a question and answer, call and response session from the Al Fann Theatrical Ensemble in Harlem with Gary Byrd as one of the teachers. In 1979 he started work on a rap called 'The Crown', about the black heritage from Egypt to West Africa to Malcolm X, Langston Hughes, Ali, Ella and Joe Louis. With music by Stevie Wonder, it was a tremendously effective use of rap which brought together much of its roots tradition and its potential.

Rap, hip-hop style, came onto the radio courtesy of Mr Magic, whose first show – 'Mr Magic's Rap Attack' – went on the air in 1979 on station WHBI, a small station in New Jersey on which you buy your own time and then sell your own commercials. This was the same station on which The World's Famous Supreme Team, the duo that can be heard on Malcolm McLaren's *Duck Rock* album (phone-in rapping over T-Ski Valley's 'Catch The Beat'), hosted their own show. With their single, 'Hey D.J.', The Supreme Team joined the long line of radio jocks and rappers who have graduated from playing other people's records to making their own. There is also a tradition of recording homages to disc jockeys. In the same spirit as Bobby Day's 'Rockin' Robin' (a 1958 tribute to a radio jock) the Brooklyn group Whodini released 'Magic's Wand' to salute Mr Magic, the jock from their own borough whose Rap Attack show had progressed from WHBI onto WBLS, the station programmed by Frankie Crocker and said to be the most listened to in America. Rap was back on the radio.

5. Sister brother rapp

The Reverend J. D. Montgomery is beginning to build his sermon at Mt Carmel Baptist Church on Detroit's east side. His theme is 'God's Newspaper' and as the pace begins to quicken he develops his striking image. The congregation, whom he describes as 'God's paperboys', are responding to every phrase with a chorus of 'yeahs' as the pastor weaves in a counterattack on young blacks who reject the Bible as a white people's book. It seems doubtful that a paper edited by the Holy Spirit with a sport section headlining Jacob wrestling an angel could displace heroes like Sugar Ray Leonard, but the power of sermons like 'God's Newspaper' is undeniable. By the time the organ and drums have joined in, the Reverend is roaring and tearing up and the people are shouting.

In another recorded sermon, the Reverend Willie T. Sneed begins his metaphor of the dead-end street haltingly, his voice pious and the congregation murmuring their responses. Again, as the song begins to form, Willie is hoarse and the flock are screaming. In his book *Black Music of Two Worlds*, John Storm Roberts writes: 'The "spiritual" sermon normally begins in a conversational tone, differentiated from white sermons only by the responses of the congregation, reminiscent of the old African belief that it is discourteous to listen dumbly, without response, or of the interjections made during the griot's telling of traditional tales.'

The power of oratory in Afro-American religion has been the foundation of the soul rap, a style of spoken song which should be seen as one of the forerunners of hip-hop rapping. The preachers like Aretha Franklin's father, the Reverend C. L. Franklin; the gospel storytellers like Dorothy Norwood with her spoken tales such as 'The Denied Mother', described by Tony Heilbut in *The Gospel Sound* as part of a 'long line of gospel records about ungrateful children and put-upon mothers'; the songs of Edna Gallman Cooke with their brief sermonettes – 'Somebody Touched Me' and 'Walk Through the Valley' – are all links in a chain which joins Marion Williams's 'The Moan That Keeps Homes Together' to Millie Jackson, Isaac Hayes, James Brown and Melle Mel's religious rap in The Furious Five's 'You Are'.

Soul rapping became such a fad in the early 1970s that one preacher, Richard 'Mr Clean' White, an ex-street gang member from New Orleans, felt compelled to claim back some lost ground, albeit 10 years too late. His sermon called 'You Got To Believe' on Savoy namechecks Isaac Hayes, Barry White, James Brown and Lou Rawls but, in a clear case of slamming the stable door after the horse had bolted, claims that 'somebody ought to rap about Jesus'.

Soul raps existed long before they became a money spinner, of course, for the simple reason that many soul singers had come out of the church. Johnnie Taylor, for instance, a singer with a half-rapped preacher-style delivery, sang lead as a replacement for

Sam Cooke in the renowned gospel group The Soul Stirrers. Songs like 'It's Cheaper To Keep Her' and 'I'd Rather Drink Muddy Water' use a conversational rap to introduce the song, and in one of his best recordings, 'I've Been Born Again', the idea is extended into a street rap complete with traffic noise as Johnnie turns down yet another night out with the boys in favour of his new love affair.

Soul raps are effective because they give the illusion of a direct and intimate communion between the singer and each individual listener. Different singers use the confessional in different ways. The grainy-voiced Laura Lee, one of the pioneers of soul rapping, used raps partly to heighten drama – in songs like 'Guess Who I Saw Today' (from her second Hot Wax album *Two Sides of Laura Lee*) dropping into speech to instil extra emotion into a line or to portray her half of a conversation. Laura Lee was also important for suggesting raps as a means by which women could voice a new independence (or at least the struggle to attain it). Songs like 'Dirty Man' and 'Uptight Good Man' suggested that the powerful female voices of black music were asking to be recognised as the voices of human beings with complex needs and qualities – not just as sets of vocal chords, lust objects or mother surrogates.

Laura Lee's precedent was followed up by a number of women. Irma Thomas, a Louisiana-born singer, recorded a stunning world-weary, men-weary rap called 'Coming From Behind (Monologue)' on the Fungus label, produced by Jerry 'Swamp Dogg' Williams. One of the clearest examples of the way in which the sermon format had been absorbed into soul music, 'Coming From Behind', released in 1973, begins with an extended rap about men, their incapacity to love and their sexual in-

I'VE BEEN BORN AGAIN: JOHNNIE TAYLOR
Photo: courtesy of Charlie Gillett

WOMEN'S LOVE RIGHTS: LAURA LEE
Photo: courtesy of Charlie Gillett

feriority, then slips into the song and ends with Irma screaming over the hypnotic backing.

Joe Tex touched on some of the same subject matter, albeit with a witty cynicism, in a rapped extension of Burt Bacharach and Hal David's 'I'll Never Fall In Love Again', included on his 1972 album *From the Roots Came the Rapper*. Tex, who died in 1982, was one of the philosophers of rap. His 'I Had a Good Home, Part Two' switches from rap to singing and back, warning you to hold on to what you've got and learn from your mistakes. As Cliff White so aptly put it in his *New Musical Express* obituary: 'Joe's quirky delivery, couched midway between benevolent preacher and lecherous uncle, gave the performance an ambiguous quality.' Starting out his career by winning a talent show with a comedy sketch, his raps also hovered on the edge of being stand-up comic routines. The same ambivalence can be found in many soul raps – in most instances they exist in the context of songs, drawing on preaching, comedy and soap-opera drama.

Lou Rawls's 'Dead End Street' is a case in point. Lou pushes home the moral of a serious story by throwing in jokes about Chicago's razor-sharp wind, the Hawk. Rawls was another gospel graduate, having started out in The Pilgrim Travellers, and he was among the first to popularise monologues with his *Live* album back in the middle '60s. The raps served to show that soul was a new kind of music with one shiny shoe in a shouting heaven and the other striding out into the material (and sexual) world.

A contemporary of Joe Tex and Lou Rawls who embodied the age-old split between the Devil and Christ was Solomon Burke. He even recorded a song called 'I Feel A Sin Coming On' as if sex was like

I'LL NEVER FALL IN LOVE AGAIN: JOE TEX
Photo: courtesy of Charlie Gillett

I FEEL A SIN COMING ON: SOLOMON BURKE
Photo: courtesy of Charlie Gillett

catching the flu. Solomon's powerful, smokey delivery is heard at its best testifying effect on a song like 'The Price', with its rapped intro stringing together the titles of his earlier recordings. In a story of such despair as 'The Price' the effect is perilously close to gimmickry, and raps can certainly skate close to bathos at times. The most risky but often the most affecting and genuinely moving are conversation raps. The implied voyeurism of overhearing somebody else's domestic squabbles is enough in itself to cause a nervous laugh – not to mention the theatricality of the whole device. A long heart-to-heart rap like Harold Melvin and the Blue Notes's 'Be For Real' completely washes out any doubts through the intensity of lead vocalist Teddy Pendergrass's searing performance. The same is true of The Soul Children's 'What's Happening Baby': John Blackfoot Colbert's voice is so full of hurt and confusion that it becomes almost painful to listen to. When it comes, his singing voice is a relief – the spoken voice cuts too close to the bone.

The moral message of 'Be For Real' – semi-religious, remember your roots, stay humble – is at the heart of many spellbinding recordings by Bobby Womack. Bobby began singing gospel with his brothers, who came to record secular material as The Valentinos, and eventually launched out on a solo career. With a singing style that could move from conversational to a hoarse shout in the space of a word, Bobby Womack has made a monologue style all his own. Maybe tracks like 'Monologue/They Long To Be Close To You' from his 1971 *Communication* album walk a thin line with their down-home wisdom, but they avoid mawkishness and manage to convince through the sheer force of personality in his voice. In another long rap medley, 'Facts of Life/He'll Be There When the Sun Goes Down', the title track from a 1973 album, he even raises the question of why he talks before he sings. It doesn't really get answered but the general conclusion – that in the midst of the entertainment circus 'it's all about feelings' – seems to sum up his music.

Despite Lou Rawls, Irma Thomas and Bobby Womack using the word *monologue* to describe their raps they were more like conversational style mixed in with songs. Monologues do exist in black music but they are far more prevalent in country music, with narrators like Red Sovine and Tex Ritter. Two black music monologues that stand out are 'Jack, That Cat Was Clean' by the mysterious Dr Horse, a story of sharp-dressing Bobo which draws heavily on the storytelling heritage of toasts, and 'King Heroin', a trenchantly eerie anti-drug rap by James Brown.

These were exceptions, though, and in the main, raps and monologues were an essential, if peripheral, aspect of deep soul. Records like Jimmy Lewis's 'Stop Half Loving These Women', Mattie Moultrie's 'The Saddest Story Ever Told', The Sons of Truth's 'Give It Up', Gwen McCrae's 'Starting All Over Again', George Kerr's 'Hey George (the masquerade is over)', Little Johnny Taylor's 'All I Want Is You' and Tami Lynn's 'Wings Upon Your Horns' are all excellent examples of the ways in which raps fit into soul.

It was three singers in the 1970s who

raided deep soul for its rapping and crossed it over to a broad international audience, making themselves stars in the process. Barry White, Isaac Hayes and Millie Jackson all had fairly established careers before they turned to the raps and monologues that gave them their notoriety. With Barry White, a west coast arranger and producer gone solo, it was a case of making the most of a limited vocal range. White growled and rumbled his way through romantic epics like 'Love Serenade' in a visionary haze of satin sheets. With a passion that threatened to rend his monstrous frame, his appeal was limitless as a focus for unexpressed sexual fantasies.

White's music appeared to be influenced by Isaac Hayes, a masterful writer and studio musician who found himself with a runaway success in *Hot Buttered Soul*, an album recorded in 1969 for Stax. It was a radical departure for soul music, obviously created by a musician accustomed to the studio and arranging. Its extended rap on 'By The Time I Get to Phoenix' – all 18 minutes of it – was a hypnotic and compelling story that built with a cinematic scope and perspective more familiar from white producers like Phil Spector and Brian Wilson. Other Ike Hayes raps like 'Monologue: Ike's Rap 1' from the *To Be Continued* album explored this compulsive area of bitter-sweet romantic tragedy further, and a whole new audience of soft-centred symphonic soul fans was created.

The singer who has developed monologues most consistently over a long period is Millie Jackson. With the ubiquitous church upbringing and a tremendously strong and expressive voice, Millie gave every impression of following in the footsteps of Aretha Franklin or Carla Thomas, but with *Caught Up*, her fourth album, she embarked on a vinyl soap opera which was so massively popular that she has pursued ideas from it ever since. The central song on *Caught Up* was a lengthy rap framed by one of the great soul ballads, '(If Loving You Is Wrong) I Don't Want To Be Right', previously recorded by Luther Ingram. The rap was a *tour de force* – a breakdown of the pros and cons of having an affair with a married man – and on the next track, 'All I Want Is a Fighting Chance', Millie confronted the wife in a playlet which continued on the follow-up album. *Still Caught Up* used rapping on almost every track and

THE ROYAL RAPPERS: ISAAC HAYES AND MILLIE JACKSON
Photo: courtesy of Stuart Cosgrove

repeated the mini-dramas of its predecessor but with the complete 'love triangle' battling it out. By the end, Millie is being carried out screaming in a straitjacket.

It was an ominous sign in more ways than one and though she returned to more conventional (if less powerful) albums subsequently, the extended raps became the focus of her stage shows. As they gradually introduced more supposedly taboo material – much of it taking the lead from Laura Lee's 'Women's Love Rights' – they also slipped into formula and self-parody. As Millie Jackson herself admitted, the monologues had become a trap which prevented her from fulfilling her potential as a singer.

Another singer who believed in confrontation tactics when approaching love triangles was Shirley Brown, who got straight on the phone to her old man's friend Barbara in 'Woman to Woman'. One of the most effective 'telephone' raps, 'Woman to Woman' was a gorgeous performance which raised the question of who-owns-who in a marriage, also pursued in Richard 'Dimples' Fields's and Betty Wright's bitter row in 'She's Got Papers On Me' and Barbara Mason's response, 'She's Got the Papers But I've Got the Man'. Betty Wright's outburst in 'She's Got Papers On Me' – 'use my life up, use my body up' – showed that there were areas in which speech could say what singing couldn't.

With raps growing out of the gospel-drenched melodramas of deep soul it was no surprise that disco was too awkward a medium for monologues to flourish. Its tempos were too fast and its mood was too optimistic. Lolleata Holloway kept the faith, though, with her scorching voice as strong on fast raps like 'All About the Paper' as it was on ecstatic shouters like 'Catch Me On the Rebound'.

In 1983–84, with the revival of interest in traditional soul, raps became fashionable again, appearing on Barbara Mason's 'Another Man', its answer – 'Another Man Is Twice As Nice' – by Tout Sweet, Fatback's 'Is This the Future', Cameo's 'She's Strange', Rich Cason's 'Street Symphony' and a host of others.

The older monologue style nearly always used speech rhythms which, though they might have more cadence to them than a lot of white speech, were not strictly related to the beat of the underlying music. In contrast, the new soul raps showed the influence of hip hop in sticking close to the drums. Some of the old-style rappers had shown an awareness of hip hop and recorded one-off singles which were premonitions of

GET ON THE GOOD FOOT: JAMES BROWN AND THE FAMOUS FLAMES *Photo: courtesy of Stuart Cosgrove*

this new hybrid – Millie Jackson released an embarrassing attack on rap, welfare scroungers and white women who go with black men. It would have been better left in the tape vaults.

James Brown, on the other hand, put together a glorious rap, 'Rapp Payback (Where Iz Moses)', that was a welcome return to records like 'Brother Rapp' and 'I Don't Want Nobody To Give Me Nothing'. It was a forceful jog to the memory. Brown was the most direct connection between soulful testifying and Bronx poetry. Though he could sing the pants off the average vocalist (as he frequently chose to prove with renditions of songs like 'If I Ruled the World'), many of his best performances existed in a unique vocal space somewhere between speech and scream. His position as spokesman for black consciousness and minister of super-heavy funk might have been on the wane by the '70s, but for the b boys he was still Soul Brother Number One.

ROXY SIDEWALK

ROXY
TOO HOT!

6. Uptown throwdown

Saturday night at The Roxy on West 18th. Trouble Funk, the heaviest of heavy funk 'n' rap groups from the Washington go-go scene, are just finishing a marathon set which runs the gamut of modern black music. Each number lasts around 30 minutes – segues of their own releases, 'Pump Me Up', 'Drop the Bomb', 'Trouble Funk Express', intercut with quotes from 'Alexander's Ragtime Band', 'Atomic Dog', 'Work That Sucker To Death', *The Munsters* theme, Taana Gardner's 'Heartbeat', Kraftwerk's 'Trans-Europe Express', all powered by the rock-hard drumming of Mack Carey. The dancers are going crazy as the group chant 'drop the bomb on the white boy too', forming a circle and challenging one another's moves. The last note dies and they file off the stage. Afrika Bambaataa, the imposing presence on the DJ platform, drops the needle onto Michael Jackson's 'P.Y.T.', the sweetest dance tune from *Thriller*.

Bambaataa may look mean when he's at the turntables but he also looks comfortable. A large man, dressed casually in sweatshirt and trainers, his image could be described as homely – certainly a million miles from the sci-fi warrior of his publicity pictures. He has a reputation for being iconoclastic in his record choices and there is no doubt that 'P.Y.T.' is a shock to the system after 90 minutes of Trouble Funk's intense bombardment of comic-strip and electronic images. The atmosphere lightens up and Bam gets to work with Soul Sonic's scratch DJ, Jazzy Jay.

Two days later, in Arthur Baker's new studio, Shakedown Sound, Bambaataa is being uncharacteristically vehement about Tommy Boy Records boss Tom Silverman's reluctance to have Soul Sonic Force and Shango sharing the same stage in the in-production movie *Beat Street*. His more usual soft-spoken manner and apparent awkwardness belie his importance as a figurehead for many black youths in the Bronx and a pioneer in the roots development and eventual international success of hip hop. His name is taken from a nineteenth-century Zulu chief (it means Chief Affection) and, ironically enough, it was

TROUBLE FUNK AT THE ROXY

RENEGADES OF FUNK: JAZZY JAY AND AFRIKA BAMBAATAA

the British film *Zulu* which gave him the idea in the early 1960s to form the Zulu Nation, a loose organisation dedicated to peace and survival which has since spread outwards from the Bronx to other parts of America. Bambaataa outlines the development:

> The Zulu Nation. I got the idea when I seen this movie called *Zulu* which featured Michael Caine. It was showing how when the British came to take over the land of the Zulus how the Zulus fought to uphold their land. They were proud warriors and they was fighting very well against bullets, cannons and stuff. They fought like warriors for a land which was theirs. When the British thought they'd won the next thing you see is the whole mountain full with thousands of Zulus and the British knew they was gonna die then. But the Zulus chanted – praised them as warriors and let them live. So from there that's when I decided one of these days I hope to have a Zulu Nation too.
>
> And then, as the years went by, through all the civil rights movement, human rights, Vietnam war and all the folk and rock that was happening – all the change of the '60s that was happening to the whole world – it just stayed with me to have some type of group like that.

Bambaataa was once a member of The Black Spades, the largest black gang in New York. Although he concedes that the gang era was tough he determinedly looks on the positive side:

> To me, the gangs was educational – it got me to learn about the streets, and The Black Spades they had a unity that I couldn't find elsewhere. I've been in a lot of different gang groups but The Black Spades had a unity among each other. The gang was like your family. You learned about how to travel around the New York streets. A lot of times when there were no jobs for youths, no trips happening in the Community Centres so the gangs got them there. If the gangs, 'scuse the expression, tore shit up, the government would start sending people to speak to you, throwing in money to

calm the gangs down. America is raised on violence. Only time America really listens is when somebody starts getting violent back.

His downplaying of gang warfare is a response to what he sees as the media's thirst for negative stories and sensationalism. That notwithstanding, the gangs escalated their rivalry to a frightening level of violence between 1968 and 1973. This internal destructiveness can only have contributed to their demise in 1974. Bambaataa puts it down to pressures from the City, drugs and the reaction of women against the fighting among the men.

In his classic study of a black Chicago gang of the '60s, the Vice Lord Nation, R. Lincoln Keiser documents the changes that caused the gang to evolve from a social group into an organised fighting gang and latterly, under the influence of Black Nationalism, into a community group:

> The club was now legally incorporated, and had received a substantial grant from government sources to undertake self-help projects. The group had started a restaurant called 'Teen Town', begun an employment service, and opened a recreation centre called 'House of Lords'. They had entered into agreements with both the Cobras and the Roman Saints, and all three of the clubs had co-operated in community help projects. The Vice Lords were strongly involved in Black pride and Black consciousness programs. A staff of both Whites and Blacks was working in the Vice Lord office on legal problems faced by members of the Lawndale community.

To outsiders the gangs may have seemed like uncontrolled mayhem but each gang had its own structure, method of operation and recognised leaders. Bambaataa joined a division of The Black Spades formed at Bronx River Project in 1969. Through the influence of his mother his main interest was music, but he was also aware of politics within the black community:

> In the '60s, that's when I was young and I was seeing a lot of things that was happening around the world. What got me excited first was when James Brown came out with 'Say It Loud, I'm Black and I'm Proud'. That's when we transcend from negro to black. Negro to us was somebody who needed to grow into a knowledge of themself. There was no land called negroland. Everbody in America – when they came here they knew what country they was from. If you were Italian you called yourself Italian-American, but the blacks didn't know which way they was going. They was brainwashed – all this stuff was put into our mentality. Black was evil, turn the other cheek, believe all the stuff that the Bible is telling you. The Bible contradicts itself. So Martin Luther King was the thing that was happening because he was fighting for civil rights, but Malcolm X was more on the aggressive side. Myself, I was more on the Malcolm X way of thinking. I respect Martin Luther King for what he was doing.

> The '60s was a beautiful time because that's when you saw change – not just in America but happening all around the world. I was watching all of that and then later when gangs was fading out I decided to get into the Nation of Islam. It put a big change on me. It got me to respect people even though they might not like us because we was Muslims. The Nation of Islam was doing things that America had been trying to for a while – taking people from the streets like junkies and prostitutes and cleaning them up. Rehabilitating them like the jail system wasn't doing.

Bambaataa's dream of having his own Zulu Nation had to wait until the gang scene had faded. While still in high school he started a group called The Organisation which lasted for two years, and with the emergence of the hip-hop scene he changed the name to the Zulu Nation:

> There were five members and we used to call them Zulu Kings. They were breakdancers. They were taking out a lot of talent that was happening in high schools and clubs and winning trophies and then more people wanted to join. As we kept playing from place to place more people came and joined and it got large like that. It started stretching from the Bronx to Manhattan, Yonkers, upstate New York to Connecticut to a lot of other places. When people used to leave and go to other states they'd build Zulu Nations according to their own way of thinking.

MR BIGGS

Mr Biggs, one of the rappers in Soul Sonic Force, the group who hit big with 'Planet Rock', backtracks to their beginnings in hip hop:

> I was rapping before the Zulu Nation even started. I started rapping back in about 1974 – just me and Bambaataa and a guy by the name of Cowboy (not the one that's with Grandmaster Flash), and this girl called Queen Kenya. Bam had just been given a new DJ set for a graduation present when he got out of high school and he started spinning records. I just picked up a mike one time, just playing around rapping, and I just kept rapping from there.

In those early days each DJ was strong in his own district and was supported by local followers. Few had access to the big clubs so the venues were block parties and schools or, in the summer, the parks. A party in the park would entail wiring the sound system to a lamp post or going to the house nearest the park, paying the owner and running a cable to their electricity. Then the party could go on until the police broke it up. DJs like Kool Dee, Flowers, Pete DJ Jones, Maboya and Smokey were all popular at the time, but for many partygoers the attention shifted to a Jamaican jock called Kool DJ Herc.

Initially, Herc was trying out his reggae records but since they failed to cut ice he switched to Latin-tinged funk, just playing the fragments that were popular with the dancers and ignoring the rest of the track. The most popular part was usually the percussion break. In Bambaataa's words: 'Now he took the music of like Mandrill, like 'Fencewalk', certain disco records that had funky percussion breaks like The Incredible Bongo Band when they came out with 'Apache' and he just kept that beat *going*. It might be that certain part of the record that everybody waits for – they just let their inner self go and get wild. The next thing you know the singer comes back in and you'd be mad'.

A conga or bongo solo, a timbales break or simply the drummer hammering out the beat – these could be isolated by using two copies of the record on twin turntables and playing the one section over and over, flipping the needle back to the start on one while the other played through. The music made in this way came to be known as beats or break beats.

Break-beat music and the hip-hop culture were happening at the same time as the emergence of disco (in 1974 known as *party music*). Disco was also created by DJs in its initial phase, though these tended to be club jocks rather than mobile party jocks – records by Barry White, Eddie Kendricks and others became dancefloor hits in New York clubs like Tamberlane and Sanctuary and were crossed over onto radio by Frankie Crocker at station WBLS. There were many parallels in the techniques used by Kool DJ Herc and a pioneering disco DJ like Francis Grasso, who worked at Sanctuary, as they used similar mixtures and superimpositions of drumbeats, rock music, funk and African records. For less creative disco DJs, however, the ideal was to slip-cue smoothly from the end of one

record into the beginning of the next. They also created a context for the breaks rather than foregrounding them, and the disco records which emerged out of the influence of this type of mixing tended to feature long introductions, anthemic choruses and extended vamp sections, all creating a tension which was released by the break. Breakbeat music simply ate the cherry off the top of the cake and threw the rest away.

In the words of DJ Grandmaster Flash:

> Disco was brand new then and there were a few jocks that had monstrous sound systems but they wouldn't dare play this kind of music. They would never play a record where only two minutes of the song was all it was worth. They wouldn't buy those type of records. The type of mixing that was out then was blending from one record to the next or waiting for the record to go off and wait for the jock to put the needle back on.

Flash has become world famous through Sugarhill releases like 'The Message', yet Herc faded from view despite his innovations in both mixing and rapping. Part of the reason for his demise was a fight at the Executive Playhouse in which he intervened and was stabbed, yet Flash also claims he had limitations as a mixer:

> Herc really slipped up. With the monstrous power he had he couldn't mix too well. He was playing little breaks but it would sound so sloppy. I noticed that the mixer he was using was a GLI 3800. It was a very popular mixer at that time. It's a scarcity today but it's still one of the best mixers GLI ever made. At the time he wasn't using no cueing. In other words, the hole was there for a headphone to go in but I remember he never had headphones over his ears. All of a sudden, Herc had headphones but I guess he was so used to dropping the needle down by eyesight and trying to mix it that from the audio part of it he couldn't get into it too well.

Herc's sound system was so powerful that when he held a block party nobody tried to compete. He would even occasionally shame Flash in public, demonstrating the superiority of his set-up over Flash's home-made rig. Grandmaster Flash's entry into mixing stemmed both from his fascination for his father's record collection and his mother's desire for him to study electronics:

> My father – he was a record collector. I think what really made me interested into wanting to get into records was because I used to get scolded for touching his records. When I was living in this town up in the Bronx called Throgs Neck he used to have this closet and in this closet were some of the classics. I mean like Benny Goodman, Artie Shaw, all the popular stuff of the time. He would close it but sometimes he would forget to lock it. He would always tell my mother, 'Don't let Joseph go in there and touch the records'. So what I would do – when my mother's back was turned or she was in the kitchen I would tiptoe up to the closet, turn the knob, go inside the closet and take a record. I would attempt to turn the stereo on. The stereo had a little red light at the bottom of the speaker and

that red light really intrigued me. Every time I'd get caught I'd get scolded or I'd get beat. Think I learned my lesson? Hell no!

I was in this place called Grier School, Hope Farm, New York upstate, where I had to stay when my mother had gotten sick. Up there they wanted parental advice on what you wanted your son or daughter to be into, so my mother chose electronics because I always had a knack of tinkering with things and taking things apart.

From there, I came out of Grier School and my mother put me into Samuel Gompers vocational high school in the Bronx there, 147th Street and Southern Boulevard. From there I caught the knack of dealing with televisions, hi-fi stereo and stuff, and that's where I really started to get a love for *sound*. We grew up underprivileged so we didn't really have the money for me to get a really nice sound system for my room. I'd get stuff that was half-disabled and put it back the best way I possibly can.

Flash was one of the first to pick upon Herc's break-beat music which, after less than a year, was becoming the dominant style in the Bronx. He began by playing records for small parties on Fox Street or Hoe Avenue, Faile Street, where there were a few empty apartments. The music was Jimmy Castor, Barry White, James Brown, Sly and the Family Stone and The Jackson Five. As his popularity grew he became aware of his own inability to synchronise beats:

I was in the experimentation phase of trying to lock the beat together. I had to be able to hear the other turntable before I mixed it over. This is when I met Pete DJ Jones. He was a big tall guy, six and some change – he was a sit-down DJ but his knees was like HUGE. I'm saying to myself, wow, how can he take these records and blend them on time, keep this music going without missing a beat? So, I finally got the heart to ask him if I could play on his system. I think he told me no twice. Then after a while he'd heard about me playing for the kids and he gave me permission to play on his system. He told me what to do and to my amazement, wow, you can actually hear the other turntable before you play it out to the people.

I knew what it was because I was going to the technical school for electronics. I knew that inside the unit it was a single pole, double throw switch, meaning that when it's in the centre it's off. When it's to the left you're listening to the left turntable and when it's to the right you're listening to the right turntable. I had to go to the raw parts shop downtown to find me a single pole double throw switch, some crazy glue to glue this part to my mixer, an external amplifier and a headphone. What I did when I had all this soldered together, I jumped for joy – I've got it, I've got it, I've got it!

I knew how to blend. Right away, when I got on Pete's set, I know how to blend. That just came naturally. My main objective was to take small parts of records and, at first, keep it on time, no

tricks, keep it on time. I'm talking about very short beats, maybe 40 seconds, keeping it going for about five minutes, depending on how popular that particular record was.

After that, I mastered punch phasing – taking certain parts of a record where there's a vocal or drum slap or a horn. I would throw it out and bring it back, keeping the other turntable playing. If this record had a horn in it before the break came down I would go – BAM, BAM, BAM-BAM – just to try this on the crowd.

The crowd, they didn't understand it at first but after a while it became a thing. After I became popular with it I wanted to get more popular, but a lot of places where they heard *of* me I would ask them if I could get on their turntables. A few clubs I used to go to, even Disco Fever, they'd say, 'No man, I heard you be scratching up people's records, man. I heard you get a wild crowd too, man. You ain't playing on my set.'

A scratch is *nothing* but the back-cueing that you hear in your ear before you push it out to the crowd. All you have to know is mathematically how many times to scratch it and when to let it go – when certain things will enhance the record you're listening to. For instance, if you're playing a record with drums – horns would sound nice to enhance it so you get a record with horns and slip it in at certain times.

A large part of the disc jockeys' mystique and power is their resourcefulness in finding unknown or obscure records that can move a crowd. These can be rarities, white-label pre-releases, acetates, unreleased tapes or simply good songs which slipped through the net at the time they were released. Given the obvious difficulty of identifying tunes in the non-stop collages of the b boy style, the most creative DJs in the Bronx were able to build up strong local reputations as 'masters of records' – the librarians of arcane and unpredictable sounds that few could match. In time-honoured fashion their secrecy extended to soaking records in the bath to peel off the centre labels or giving records new names. Previously jealously guarded lists, emerging gradually at the beginning of 1984, make bizarre reading. Bambaataa was one of the most outrageous:

The Bronx wasn't really into radio music no more. It was an anti-disco movement. Like you had a lot of new wavers and other people coming out and saying, 'Disco sucks'. Well, the same thing with hip hop, 'cos they was against the disco that was being played on the radio. Everybody wanted the funky style that Kool Herc was playing. Myself, I was always a record collector and when I heard this DJ, I said, 'Oh, I got records like that.' I started digging in my collection.

When I came on the scene after him I built in other types of records and I started getting a name for master of records. I started playing all forms of music. Myself, I used to play the weirdest stuff at a party. Everybody just thought I was crazy. When everybody was going crazy I would throw a commercial on to cool them out – I'd throw on *The Pink Panther* theme for everybody who thought they was cool like the Pink Panther, and then I would play 'Honky Tonk Woman' by The Rolling Stones and just keep that beat going. I'd play something from metal rock records like Grand Funk Railroad. 'Inside Looking Out' is just the bass and drumming . . . rrrrrmmmmmmm . . . and everybody starts freaking out.

I used to like to catch the people who'd say, 'I don't like rock. I don't like Latin.' I'd throw on Mick Jagger – you'd see the blacks and the Spanish just *throwing* down, dancing crazy. I'd say, 'I thought you said you didn't like rock.' They'd say, 'Get out of here.' I'd say, 'Well, you just danced to The Rolling Stones.' 'You're kidding!'

I'd throw on 'Sergeant Pepper's Lonely Hearts Club Band' – just that drum part. One, two, three, BAM – and they'd be screaming and partying. I'd throw on The Monkees, 'Mary Mary' – just the beat part where they'd go 'Mary, Mary, where are you going?' – and they'd start going crazy. I'd say, 'You just danced to The Monkees'. They'd say, 'You liar. I didn't dance to no Monkees'. I'd like to catch people who categorise records.

Through listening to the type of records that were popular in the beginnings of hip hop (and have remained popular) it becomes easier to understand how the better-known aspects of the culture – rapping, scratching, beat-box music – came to evolve. A b boy classic like James Brown's 'Get Up, Get Into It, Get Involved', released in late 1970, is an up-tempo call and answer routine between Brown and singer Bobby Byrd. For most whites at the time, this was the most meaningless type of James Brown release, but for those young blacks still living in areas like the Bronx and Harlem every phrase had a message.

The record is a single, harsh, see-sawing guitar riff with the bass rumbling upfront in the mix and the drummer playing loose funk with the hi-hat cymbal opened then choked shut on the fourth beat of the bar. There is no bridge: the only change in the structure comes half-way through, with a drum break where James shouts, 'Fellers, I want you to hit me.' the band shout back 'Yeah' and the horns hit, 'Hit me' . . . BAM . . . 'Alright, hit me' . . . BAM . . . 'Hey' . . . BAM.

The effect is identical to the kind of punch phasing using horns over drum tracks that can be heard on bootlegs of b boy parties. The break is followed by a tortured rock guitar solo and at the end Brown shouts the prophetic, 'You can be like a tape deck, you know . . . they can plug you in . . . say what they want you to say . . . don't let 'em do it'. The last phrase is repeated four times, with Bobby Byrd shouting back a resist and survive NO each time.

Most of the words – phrases like 'get an education' and 'do it one time . . . get it right' – are shouted or rapped over the music, with Brown's voice rising to a scream towards the close. The general message – a positive exhortation not to waste your life or be manipulated by others – was part of a series of records which encouraged black youth to stay in school, avoid succumbing to hard drugs and be proud of the colour of their skin.

The other important break-beat records had some or all of the same ingredients – a funky beat, a positive message, a drum break and some rock guitar: Jimmy Castor's 'It's Just Begun', Rufus Thomas's 'Do the Funky Penguin' and 'The Breakdown', Baby Huey and the Babysitters' 'Listen To Me', The Isley Brothers' 'Get Into Something' and Dyke and the Blazers' 'Let a Woman Be a Woman – Let a Man Be a Man'. Other records with drum breaks that could be used to construct new tunes were 'Johnny The Fox Meets Jimmy the Weed' by Thin Lizzy (released as a bootleg mix on Dirt Bag Records and called 'Johnny the Fox' by Skinny Lizzy); 'The Big Beat' by heavy-metal guitarist Billy Squire (also released as a bootleg record featuring just the opening bars of the song) and 'Scorpio' by Dennis Coffey, a white session guitarist. 'Scorpio' (an inspiration in name if nothing else to the 1982 electro track by Grandmaster Flash and the Furious Five) was included on one of Paul Winley's *Super Disco Brakes* anthologies. The first volume of *Super Disco Brakes* includes New Birth's peculiar Sly Stone-meets-psychedelia fusion, 'Gotta Get a Knutt', which can be heard on another bootleg, *Live Convention '82* (volume two), recorded at T Connection.

Live Connection '82 (Disco Wax Records) begins with an extract from 'Academy Awards', a track from Masterfleet's 1973 album *High On The Seas* featuring Star Trek actress Nichelle Nichols. After fragments of the 'Good Times' bass riff, some Sly Stone, 'Gangster Boogie' and a litany of guest DJs and MCs who are 'in the house', there is a five-minute 27-second rap which uses the first six bars (13 seconds in total) of 'Do the Funky Penguin' cut together by the Grand Wizard Theodore:

It's like a one for the treble and two for the bass
Theodore – let's dog the place
You don't stop, you don't stop, that body rock
Just clap your hands, it's the sure shot sound
Brace yourself – for the one that goes down
Got a little news that you all can tell
Theodore – he got the clientele
All night, y'all, if it's alright
All night, y'all, if it's alright
Porto Rico, Porto Rico
Make money, make money, make money into the Patty Duke
Throw your hands in the air
Wave 'em like you just don't care
Getting down with these sure-shot sounds your body say oh yeah
Yeah, a little louder, little louder
You don't stop, you don't, you won't don't don't
You won't don't don't, you don't don't stop the body rock
Because the people in the back – you ain't the wack
But – don't stop the body rock

B BOY GLOVE, THE ROXY

The people in the middle, let me see you wiggle
(but don't stop that body rock)
The people on the side – let's ride
(but don't you stop that body rock)
The girls in the rear, you come up here
(but don't you stop that body rock)
Young lady in the blue, I'm talking to you
(but don't you stop that body rock)
Young lady in the brown, you know you're down
(don't stop that body rock)
Young lady in the green, you're looking real clean
(don't you stop that body rock)
Young lady in the black, you ain't the wack
(you ain't thinking 'bout stopping that body rock)
Young lady in the white, she'll bite all night
(but don't you stop that body rock)
Young lady in the yellow got a faggot for a fellow
(but don't you stop that body rock)
'Cos the body rock is sho nuff the shot
(but you won't stop, you don't stop)
Ain't thinking 'bout stopping that body rock
Punk rock, rock the house
Patty Duke, y'all, get cute y'all
Patty Duke, y'all, get cute y'all
Gonna tell you little something, I'm one of a kind
But now I'm gonna rock – the zodiac signs

Pisces – rock the house
Aquarius – rock the house
And Gemini – said get on high
Scorpio – you're the go
Pisces – the higher degree
Just the beat beat beat, the beat beat the beat
Patty Dukeing to the rhythm, get up out your seat
Young ladies – are you with me?
Young ladies – are you with me?
Young ladies in the house say OWW
Say OWW – to the beat, y'all
You don't quit, you don't quit
You don't you don't quit quit
The sure-shot shit
It's like superstition with a bag of tricks
I say this is the way we harmonise
This is the way we turn it up
This is the way we turn it up

And the beat goes on. Raps like these, with their eulogies to the young ladies in blue, red, etc., are reminiscent of black dance music from all eras – country blues and jug bands, piano blues like 'Pinetop's Boogie Woogie', the shouters like Big Joe Turner, the electric blues of John Lee Hooker and Junior Wells, the rock 'n roll of Larry Williams and Little Richard – not great poetry but dancehall rhymes.

As has already been shown, rapping has roots in a variety of sources, but for the hip-hop purists it is again Kool DJ Herc who was the first to come up with a Bronx MC style. Bambaataa remembers:

> There's a lot of people trying to take credit like Cheeba and DJ Hollywood – the disco type of DJs that was out there – but I challenge any of these people to sit down and base their facts on when they started to do what we was doing in the street. A lot of these people who claim to be the start of it was doing rapping something like Frankie Crocker or talk like disco-style radio-type rapping. Herc took phrases, like what was happening in the streets, what was the new saying going round the high school like 'rock on my mellow', 'to the beat y'all', 'you don't stop', and just elaborated on that.

Bambaataa sees a connection between Herc's Jamaican origins and his rapping: 'He knew that a lot of American blacks were not getting into the reggae of his country. He took the same thing that they was doing – toasting – and did it with American records, Latin or records with beats.'

Rappers like Mr Biggs are more inclined to give some credit to Eddie Cheeba and DJ Hollywood for their part in the general development of rap, even though their sources were the radio rather than the schoolyard. DJ Hollywood was in fact rapping over disco records between acts at Harlem's Apollo Theatre. Kurtis Blow, whose smooth style is closer to this kind of combined DJ/MC, remembers Hollywood as the rap innovator, although the Hollywood rhyme he recites from memory is word-for-word Isaac Hayes's badman rap 'Good Love 6-9969' from his 1975 album *Use Me*. Ike's career may have been on the wane by that time, but his influence was obviously still alive in the streets.

Flash also gives Hollywood credit: 'He

was one of the greatest solo rappers that ever there was. That boy could blaze a crowd – the rhymes he says. I expected him to shoot right to the top – he had a chance before we did.' Hollywood also played at Club 371 and his style was capable of appealing to the older fans as well as the b boys.

Lil Rodney Cee, now with Double Trouble, recalls the formative years of MCs in the middle 1970s:

> The way rap is *now* – it isn't the way it was *then*. Whereas then it was just phrases; the MC would say little phrases like, 'To the Eastside, make money. To the Westside, make money', or 'To the rock, rock, rock, to the rock, rock, rock'. In '77–'78 I was with The Magnificent Seven. We was playing in the streets. Rap, then, was only a street thing. At that time, everything was happening at once. B boying was happening at the same time as DJing and rapping came out. Everything was strictly competitive.
>
> The groups that came out was in strict competition, so when we did play in the wintertime we rented small clubs, discotheques, recs, boys' clubs, PALs. We charged little bits of money and people came and that's what we did in the wintertime. With the money that we made we invested in our sound system for the summertime. That was the basic foundation of what every group did to start off and get into the rap industry.
>
> At the time it wasn't groups rapping – it was solo MCs and they would have a DJ. It would be one DJ and one MC. They would just come out and the people

DOUBLE TROUBLE AT DANCETERIA

liked it. The more they did the more it got into a unified stage. We said, 'Hey, we should get more MCs'.

Along with his partner in Double Trouble, KK Rockwell, Rodney was in one of the very first rap groups, Funky Four Plus One More. He recalls the emergence of rap styles and the competitiveness:

The first MC that I know of is Cowboy, from Grandmaster Flash and the Furious Five. He was the first MC to talk about the DJ. He would talk for Grandmaster Flash and say how great Flash is – you know, 'the pulsating, inflating, disco shaking, heartbreaking, the man on the turntable' and that's all it was. And then, to have fun, it got into – okay, everybody came from all different places to hear the music so when they came they all were into whatever they were into whether it was graffiti, dancing, b boying – the b boys were strictly in competition, too.

An uptown group would battle a downtown group. What I mean by battle is that they could come and they would say, 'Okay. Us four are better than your four', and we would go at it. We would pick one and we would dance against each other. We'd do one move and they'd do a move and the crowd liked it. That's where the competition came in. This is before any records, before any money was made. This was from our hearts.

Grandmaster Flash and the Furious Five embody the gradual move from underground to overground. Dressed in red leathers (old-style DC Comics Flash) and working his way through a pack of Lucky Spike bubblegum, Flash waxes nostalgic over the good old days. The contradictions of roots culture in the marketplace have hit very hard; five years after the first rap records and 10 years since hip hop began to stir, most groups and soloists are gathering themselves to launch out on the second phase in the music business, often with a sobering hindsight wisdom that show business can be no business at all. As a 17-year-old the chances of having good financial and legal advice are very slim. Flash is very conscious that pioneer rappers like DJ Hollywood and Busy Bee Starski have not had the breaks of other, lesser talents, and he is also depressed by the changes that have inevitably wrung the verve out of the scene as a whole. His career shows the process in microcosm:

I had to prove to myself that I could rock a crowd, so as opposed to making them pay I tried it for free. Meaning that I would go in the park and play – St Marys, 23 Park, 63 Park – these are various parks I used to play at and just do this new thing called scratching and called phasing and see if they would like it. And it just so happened that they did like it. Not knowing, all the time I was doing this, that there were people following me older men following me. They made a proposal to me: 'Flash, let's take it on the inside for a dollar or two and see how this works.'

At that time, with my mixing ability,

once I warmed up and really got into it, the crowd would stop dancing and just gather round as if it was a seminar. This was what I didn't want. This wasn't school – it was time to shake your ass. From there I knew it was important to have vocal entertainment. There were quite a few MCs, as we called it before the industry called it rap, that tried out for the job to rap with me and the first member of the crew to really pass the test was Keith Wiggins, known as Cowboy.

He had a Simon Says-ish type of style. The particular MC I was looking for was somebody who could complement scratching. This person had to be able to talk with all the obscure scratching I was doing. I'm doing all this but I'm doing it all on time so you have to have the ear to really know. Even now, I might walk into a club and if I'm cutting and keeping it going they rap, but if I stop on time to the beat they get lost. There's some that can't really catch on to it when the music's being phased in and out to the beat. Cowboy, he was superb at it. As far as that 'Ho', 'Clap your hands to the beat' and 'Say oh yeah', I'd have to give him credit for being one of the creators of that.

From there I had gotten Melvin Glover who had almost like a scholastic type of style. From there I had got Danny – he could say rhymes from now to doomsday. He was a person who run his mouth but he could also talk with the sort of obscure scratching I was doing. So it was like Grandmaster Flash and the Three MCs. It worked pretty good. From there I was ready to take it to the inside.

We tried in this club called the Back Door at 169th Street and Boston Road for a dollar. We would party from like 10 at night till 7 in the morning. When we were playing at the Back Door we had diehard fans – it was to a point where kids were sneaking out the house. I try to keep a rapport with some of my close fans and with their parents. I'd even give them the cab fare to get home after the party. I would sit down with some of the mothers and like, 'Flash, they won't go to school. They won't go to church but let them hear about you playing at the Back Door – boy, they'll get up, get dressed and they'll definitely be there'.

It was like an omen. If you don't come to a Flash party it's something you missed. If you weren't there you felt like an onion – you had to be there, even against your mother's and father's wishes. Then after a while there were crews being created – this was when crews were *really* being created seven or eight years ago. The Malachi Crew, oh, there were so many crews.

Flash's number-one fan, his minder Kevin, has a good memory for crews: 'The Casanovas, The Potheads, The Cheeba Crew, there was a crew for every block.' He also remembers some of the wilder turntable trickery of the time:

He did this shit one day that fascinated me. See, I was a devoted fan. I wasn't down with the crew – now I am. It was at Roosevelt High School or Bronx River, one of those two. Him and Mike and Disco B were doing their Terrible Trio thing. Flash would cut the record and move out of the way, then Disco B would do it then Flash would do it then Mike would do it. Then they had this other thing they did where they would pop up out of nowhere – from this angle you couldn't see them. It was a different DJ every second – 'Good times . . . good times . . . good times'. The most phenomenal was at Roosevelt. This nigger did this shit. He drop back. He fell back – I thought he'd bust his *ass*. What it was, he had kicked off his shoe and *kicked* the fader. It was perfectly on time. The crowd went *wild* – I mean, niggers was pushing and falling and shit!

Taking this kind of DJ style from community venues into the commercial world of the clubs (no matter how small) involved an inevitable growth in following. Flash recalls the nights at the Back Door:

It was a big success but it was a small place. We would open the doors at 11 o'clock, and 12 o'clock the doors would be *closed*. It was a thing where I would have to pace it. Eleven to 12.30 I would play cool-out hustle music for the calm people, the sophisticated b boy people in the place that wanted to do the hustle or dance proper. But from 1 to 2.30, that's like grab your partner 'cos I'm playing the hottest shit in the crates. My assistant pulls out the *powerful* shit – I'd set up the order according to beats-per-minute, tempo and I'd say, 'Hand it to me, man, just like that', and once I'd start playing that shit the crowd would just go. The Incredible Bongo Band, 'Bongo Rock', 'Johnny the Fox', 'The Bells' – Bob James – 'Mardi Gras'. Me watching them enjoy themselves so much I would really like 'pop pop pop pop poppoppop u u u u'. I would like break the shit down to eighth, sixteenth notes. It amazed me sometimes.

Bob James was like 102 beats-per-minute and I would go from 102 beats-per-minute to 118 so from there it was like Bob James, James Brown, Donald Byrd, Roy Ayers to John Davis and the Monster Orchestra, 'I Can't Stop', and that's like the ultimate, you know. From there I would keep it going but I would give myself a break because for about 50 minutes I'm bending down uncomfortably. I'd put on 'Dance to the Drummer's Beat', which is a fairly long break, about four minutes, let it play for a while and then play the slow jams, the real oldies. After you sweat and you're tired you appreciate it: 'Oh, he finally slowed it down.' The Delfonics, The Moments, The Five Stairsteps – the real slow, out-of-date stuff that was really love songs. I had all that stuff in my crates. I had something like 45 crates behind me.

Flash and Kevin reminisce by singing the chorus of The Delfonics' 'For the Love I Gave To You' and recalling how Flash would cut mix the same line over and over, keeping the romantic dancers going for over a minute on the same spot. Eventually,

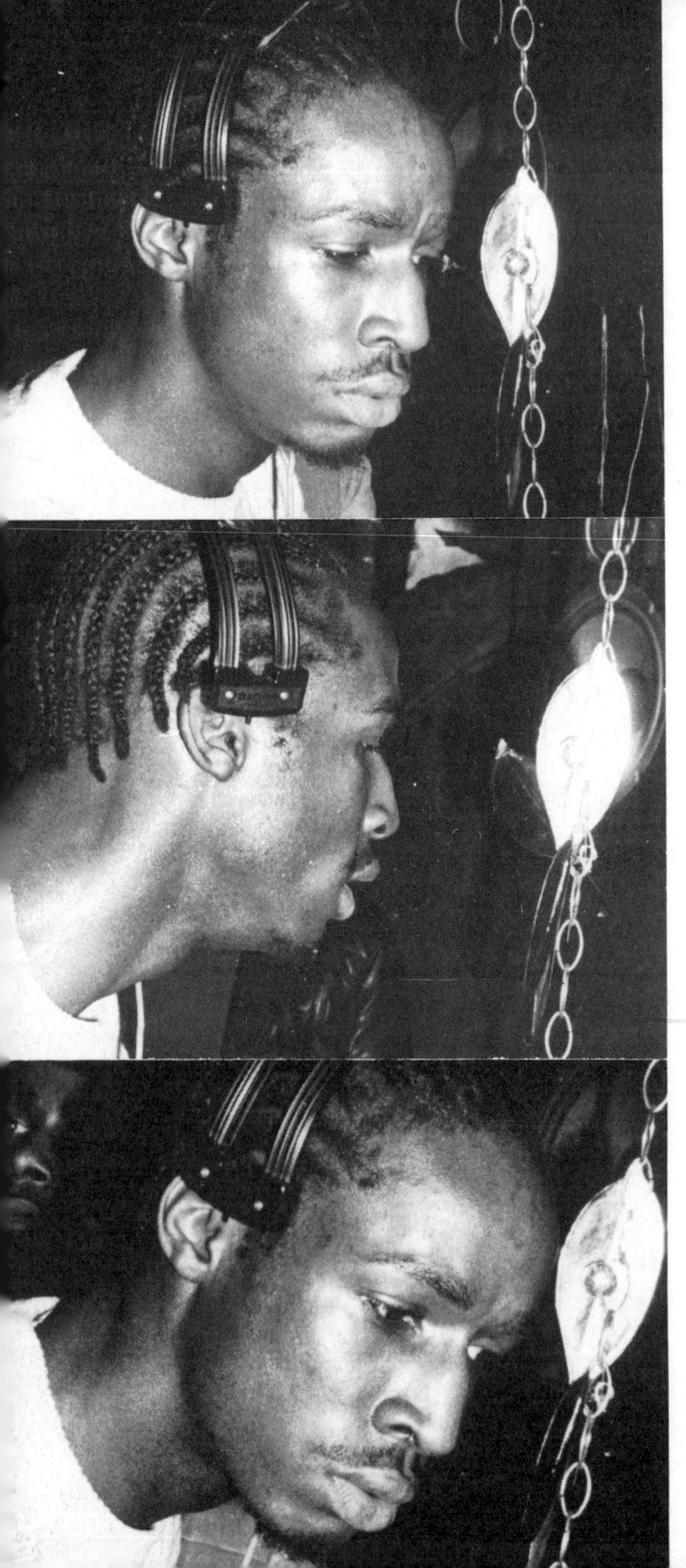

the crowd at the Back Door swelled beyond capacity to the point of discomfort:

> So it was to a point where we had to move the corporation down the block to Freeman Street. It was this place called the Dixie Club. That became our new home. The crowd got monstrous and the high school students, who had heard of me and really used to down me, they came to the parties a few times – got a taste of it – they really enjoyed that. We gave them a good time. So they would go to their school organisations and say, 'You want Flash.' After a while we started knocking all the schools off – Roosevelt, Taft, Monroe, Bronx River. It wasn't so much a party – it was a commercial thing where we were getting hired on a professional basis. By that time we had built up a pretty decent sound system.
>
> A year and a half, two years later, the pinnacle of a DJ's group's career, before it was recording, was who can make it to The Audubon. Once you've played there you are famous throughout the five boroughs. The place held 3,000 people so you're bound to get people from all over the place. It was real strange. The people who were working with me, they said, 'Flash, we've played all the schools. We're growing out of the Dixie Club. We've grown out of most gymnasiums we've played in. I want to take you to this place, Flash. I've already rated it and I'm setting it up for the next month.'

ADVENTURES ON THE WHEELS OF STEEL: GRANDMASTER FLASH AT BROADWAY INTERNATIONAL

He takes me to this building – this place is like a block and a half *long*. I said, 'No, please. Let's not try *this* step.' He says, 'Flash, there's no other place that you can try. Anything smaller than this would be a step down. Give me a month to publicise it.' After that day he showed me, I would go down there by myself for about four or five days and think, 'I'm not ready for this place. This is too big.' The Fire Department sign says '3,000 people. No More.' I said to myself, 'I'll be lucky to get 400 in this motherfucker, talk about *3,000*!'

So the night came. After a month publicising me everyone who was interested knew about this big affair. So I bring my sound system in there. It's not really powerful enough to rock this whole place but I put it up high. Strategically, if you put it up high the sound might not be strong but you can at least hear it. The night before I had come up with a way to cut without cueing and I showed it to this guy named Georgie George and Melvin. And Melvin – Melle Mel – as soon as he had seen it he made up a routine. I said, 'I'm not ready to do this shit', but it was too late. I didn't want to back out.

So the Audubon comes. Open the doors 11 o'clock. It was like 200 or 300 people. I left out 'cos I was kind of embarrassed, you know, and came back about 12.30, 1 o'clock. This place was JAM PACKED FULL! I said, 'Oh shit!' Kool DJ AJ was playing with us. He was pumping the crowd. Everybody was there – the gangsters, the scramblers, the little kids. I went downstairs – the line

was around the corner. The shit is jumping off.

We played. Melvin says, 'Stop the music' and introduces me – 'The world's greatest DJ – Grandmaster Flash'. Everybody thought I was going to do regular stuff. I went into my spinning back, turning backwards. The crowd was screaming. I said, 'I'm not gonna get nervous. If I let my emotions get to me I'm going to fuck up and it's gonna jump out of the grooves.' I'm trying to stay steady. After a while, I had to do the other thing, which is taking the needle and dropping it with no cueing at all – keeping the beat on time. It was taking one beat – dropping it and counting. This is blind – BAM – BAM – I kept it on time. I did it about 10 times. Backed off and the crowd went berserk. The fucking floor was like about to cave in. After that night I felt so good. That was September 2nd 1976.

I was ready to try that shit again. Two months later we tried it and after a while what had happened was other corporations, other b boy groups, were going in there and tearing the place up, breaking out the windows and then the news media and the cops started talking bad about it . . . 'These groups, they call themselves b boys, they're coming down to rent the place and bringing all these wild people. People are getting shot and windows are getting broken out.' So the Audubon was out. There was no super-large place that you could play in.

We was doing it with just us and one other DJ. Other groups that didn't have the heart to go in by themselves were going in there with six or seven DJ groups. Seven or eight different sound systems – it was too confusing. This person was taking too long to turn on or this person's system was fucking up and once you've got that big mass of people you have to keep them entertained. So after a while motherfuckers was getting shot and this and that, so by the time we went back after the third time our clientele was getting kind of scared so we gave it up. Then we started knocking off schools – older places, the Savoy Manor Ballroom, the Renaissance Ballroom – all the posh clubs. For three years things were going great, then all of a sudden you hear on the radio, 'To the hip hop, hippedy hop, you don't stop'. I'm saying to myself, 'I know of anybody else from here to Queens or Long Island that's doing this. Why don't I know of this group called The Sugarhill who? The Sugarhill Gang. They don't know of me and I don't know them. Who are these people?'

They got a record on the radio and that shit was haunting me because I felt we should have been the first to do it. We were the first *group* to really do this – someone took our shot. Every night I would hear this fucking record on the radio, 92KTU, 98, BLS, rock stations. I was hearing this shit in my dreams.

7. Raptivity in captivity

Until 1979 the sole documentation of Bronx hip hop was cassette tapes – either clandestine tapes made by would-be bootleggers at parties and clubs, or tapes made by the groups themselves and given out to friends, to cab drivers or to kids with giant tape boxes just to get the music out. Some, like Flash, are reputed to have sold their tapes for 'a buck a minute'.

The lack of industry connections in the Bronx, the young age group involved in hip hop and the radical primitivism of the music itself conspired to produce an island of relatively undisturbed invention in a sea of go-getter commerce. Although hip hop was an idcalistic movement it was based in self-determination – a positive and realist attitude. This was very different from the romanticism central to disco which, although uplifting, was more likely to be fixed on an upwardly mobile good life. Hip hop was raw and its environment was seen as being uniformly tough and rough, even if some of it wasn't. The young MCs who chanted about their expensive clothes, champagne, cars and apartments lived with the most minimal hope of ever possessing them; for a group like Chic, on the other hand, whose name, image and subject matter exclusively suggested a moneyed party set hard at play, the fantasy was, in a material sense at least, close to being real. Chic made an awful lot of money and though *they* might spend their time hard at work in recording studios their fans were inspired by the buoyancy and crazy optimism embodied in their dance tunes. Some of them might even have owned a car to get them home from the disco.

One of the last great records of the disco era (an era in many ways defined by a marketing concept as much as a musical form) was Chic's 'Good Times', a release which gave them twelfth place in the Cashbox top singles for 1979. Logic suggested that if these were the good times then bad times must be just around the corner. They were, of course, and the record captured that sunset feeling.

It was a studio remake of the 'Good Times' rhythm which provided the backing track for the record that came to haunt the dreams of Grandmaster Flash. 'Rapper's Delight' by The Sugarhill Gang was the first release on a new label called Sugarhill, operating out of West Street, Englewood, New Jersey. Reportedly bankrolled with a third share from the legendary Morris Levy of Roulette Records, it was the newest incarnation of a group of companies run by Sylvia Robinson and her husband Joe Robinson Sr. The co-president of this new venture and its figurehead, Sylvia was a recording artist herself. Formerly known as Sylvia Vanderpool, she recorded as Little Sylvia for Savoy Records shortly after Little Esther (Phillips) left the company for Federal in 1951. Through taking guitar lessons with Mickey Baker (now the author of a renowned jazz guitar tutor book) she came to team up with him in a duo called Mickey and Sylvia. After two years and five record releases they hit big with 'Love Is

RAPPER'S DELIGHT: THE SUGARHILL GANG

KING TIM III: PERSONALITY JOCK

Strange', a record with a marked Bo Diddley feel, a catchy guitar figure and a conversation rap in the middle. Mickey and Sylvia continued as a duo until the '60s though none of their subsequent releases took off in the same way. Mickey went on to work in France as a jazz and blues guitarist. Sylvia moved into business ventures with the Blue Morocco Club on Boston Road in the Morrisania area of the Bronx and then in 1968 formed a collection of record labels – All Platinum, Turbo, Stang and Vibration – and later bought the Chess catalogue, much to the discomfort of some of its more illustrious signings like Muddy Waters.

Of the records released on All Platinum or its subsidiaries, a surprising number are of vocal eccentrics – the quavering voice of George Kerr, the strained falsetto of Donnie Elbert, the deep soul hysterics of the great (but sadly late) Linda Jones, the truly bizarre Shirley Goodman (one half of the Shirley and Lee duo) and, not least, the breathy, half-rapped seductions of Sylvia herself on 'Pillow Talk' and 'Lay It On Me'. All Platinum also released a number of monologues by artists such as Dave 'Baby' Cortez and Enoch Gregory and found room for a Last Poets-type group called The Universal Messengers, whose records came out on Turbo. Perhaps it was this liberal attitude to vocal style that gave Sylvia an open mind to rap (as MCing came to be known after 'Rapper's Delight'). Other practices at All Platinum – their low-budget commercialism ('Girls', Moments and Whatnauts's moment of ultimate sexism with its cheap but icily effective string synthesiser); the habit of using backing tracks and tacky instrumentals for B sides (turn over 'Girls' and you get 'More Girls' – the wordless version: not such a bad thing considering the lyrics); cover versions of disco hits (Gil Scott-Heron's 'In the Bottle' redone by Brother to Brother, who then went on to cover 'Every Nigger Is a Star'), these were all revived for the new rap fad. There was even a vocal group called The Ponderosa Twins Plus One, whose unusual 'Plus One' tag pre-dated Funky Four Plus One More by some years.

There are many stories about Sylvia's first confrontation with rap. One of the most romantic is that she was taken to a niece's birthday party at Harlem Disco World and subsequently signed the group who were rapping on the mike there, naming them The Sugarhill Gang in memory of her roots across the Hudson River on Sugar Hill. Double Trouble, true to their name, have a more elaborate account which probably comes closer to the actual events. Lil Rodney Cee gives his version:

> Rap was travelling through the tapes so people was coming from Jersey who had family in New York. They'd hear the rap tapes and take them to Jersey. Somehow, Miss Robinson got an ear on what was going on. Her little kids loved rap music – they had all the rap tapes and they knew of us, The Funky Four, and Grandmaster Flash. They knew what was going on in New York. She said, 'Hey, if my kids like this all the kids around the world will like this!' So that's where she got the idea to make a record.
>
> How she picked the Gang – that's another story. Hank was a bouncer at a local club we used to play at. He used to be at the door and if there was trouble he'd throw 'em out. That was Hank's job but while he was at the door he'd learn what was going on – he learned how to rap. He was working in a pizza shop in Jersey. Miss Robinson came in the pizza shop and he was in there rapping, saying somebody else's rhymes. She said, 'You wanna make a record?' and he said, 'Sure, why not?'
>
> Mike was a friend of her older son. They went to school together. Mike was with another group that was forming out in Jersey. Master G was with a group too. At that time, being that he was a friend of her son, her son said, 'Ma, I got a friend that can rap.' He brought Mike home

DOUBLE TROUBLE

and she listened to him rap and said, 'Hey, you wanna make a record?' He said, 'Yeah.' Guy heard in the streets in Jersey that Miss Robinson was going to make a rap record and he felt that he could rap so he got in touch with her. He rapped for her and she said, 'Come on, we're gonna go in the studio.' They stayed in the studio for three days, they used Chic's record and came up with 'Rapper's Delight'.

KK Rockwell remembers his reaction to first hearing the record: 'I was walking down the block one day and it was coming out the record store speaker. I thought it was a tape. Then, I heard it was a record and I was going out of my mind. I didn't know what the world was coming to then! We was thinking of making a record at that time but we had no connections to make a record'. Financially, Sugarhill's first release was an auspicious start for the label. 'Rapper's Delight' reached number 36 in the US charts, became a huge international hit and went on to become the biggest-selling 12-inch record ever. Joey Robinson Jr (Sylvia and Joe's son, an executive in Sugarhill who was running his mother's fan club in 1977) is quoted in *Right On Focus* magazine's *Rap Music Special* of winter '83 as claiming: 'If you come up with something first, someone's gonna go with it if they like it. We couldn't keep up with the demand for the record. It was selling an average of between 50 and 60,000 a day. To this day, we're still selling copies of 'Rapper's Delight' even if it's only 100 or 200 a month, we'll still sell copies and not one return.'

Musically, the record was less thrilling. In the early days of the 12-inch single, records used the available time to the full. Ten minutes of Lolleata Holloway, Melba Moore or Bettye LaVette was an emotional epic; 14 minutes 10 seconds of non-stop rhymes from The Sugarhill Gang was more like listening to farming news or stock market reports. Although nobody knew it at the time, their verses were recycled from groups like The Cold Crush Brothers; they were to Bronx hip hop what The Police were to The Sex Pistols, the difference being that the Bronx originals had yet to find a Malcolm McLaren figure with a stack of confrontational tactics to help them out.

Although Joey Robinson Jr is right in suggesting that success came from stealing a march on everybody else, 'Rapper's Delight' was not the first rap record. Earlier in 1979, The Fatback Band released a single called 'You're My Candy Sweet' on Spring Records. The B side was given over to a rap called 'King Tim III (Personality Jock)'. New York record stores began playing the rap in preference to the rather feeble top side, and disco station WKTU followed up with airplay. Both the single and the album were surprise hits.

Like 'Rapper's Delight' the song had novelty value for the general public, even if uptown MCs were contemptuous of it. Fatback were a Brooklyn band (part of the reason why the Bronx MCs disliked them) and their unexpected rap hit was a throwback to the brilliant minimalist funk and soul brother rap of early '70s records like 'New York Style' and 'Wicki Wacky'. By 1979 they were on the downward spiral –

success with 'street' music is bound to cause problems sooner or later – and the album containing 'King Tim III' is directionless and half-hearted. Whether they were consciously or unconsciously casting around for ideas, when Fatback heard DJ Hollywood rapping on the mike between acts they were taken with the idea. Lil Rodney Cee remembers King Tim III as Fatback's master of ceremonies – 'Ladeeez and Gennelmun . . . THE FATBACK BAAAND' – though other stories portray them searching him out after hearing a tape of his rapping over Roy Ayers's 'Running Away'. Their rap and 'Running Away' do have an uncanny similarity – identical tempo, a sing-along chorus and a bass line with a melodic hook in the first three beats of each bar. Coincidence?

King Tim's contribution was a stilted mixture of old-style MC and radio rapping, peppered with a few b boy phrases. Whatever latent talent he may have had failed to materialise. After a solo release the following year, another Fatback production called 'Charley Says! (Roller Boogie Baby)', he vanished from sight. 'Charley Says' was a better record than its predecessor but by 1980 the floodgates had opened and the competition was hot.

The energy of the Bronx scene had been spreading to other areas of New York and in 1979 rapping was widespread throughout the city. It took the success of Sylvia's first steps into the field to alert other record producers that something was happening that was worth recording. Bobby Robinson of Enjoy Records regrets his own shortsightedness:

It had been around since 1976 and I was aware of it – kids walking down the street with big boxes that you'd hear blasting all over. It was the kind of a thing where you'd hear kids do it in the street – everybody would laugh. Maybe it was because I wasn't actively recording. I kick myself because I should have been the first one out with a record. My good friend Sylvia Robinson at Sugarhill came out with the first giant rap record and she didn't know from nothing until she happened to hear it. She heard it one Saturday night and she flipped.

SYLVIA AND JOE ROBINSON AT SUGARHILL RECORDS, ENGLEWOOD, NEW JERSEY

I was working with some artists, writing and regrouping and getting ready to re-launch. Then, when I saw the success of The Sugarhill Gang and how *crazy* people went over this record, I said, well, I can't wait to get into my regular line of things. I'm gonna jump on this rap thing.

Bobby Robinson's move was significant in that he had been one of the most important record producers in rhythm and blues on the eastern seaboard of America. He was often the first to spot talent and was a catalyst in the careers of many performers who are now world famous – Gladys Knight and the Pips among many others.

At midday on a Friday in 1984, Bobby's Happy House Records is saturating Harlem's 125th Street with the explosive yearning of Otis Redding's 'That's How Strong My Love Is'. A few doors east is the Apollo Theatre, currently undergoing conversion into a venue which will broadcast videos of black acts as an antidote to the barrage of mediocre rock videos on cable station MTV. Over the street is Rainbow Records and a little further you can find Paul Winley Records. Walk back west and Bobby Robinson can be found in his apartment, currently cluttered with paperwork owing to a fire at his office. This is just one of the personal problems and setbacks which beset him at the moment but there have been quite a few during the last three decades and, as before, he has plans to bounce back:

I started in 1951. I went into the music business with the retail store in 1946 and all of a sudden, for some reason, my name started to spread nationwide as the most knowledgeable guy in black music. Any information you wanted – check with Bobby Robinson. The Apollo Theatre being only half a block from my place I met everybody in the black music business and a considerable amount of white artists who came from time to time as well. Everybody started to call me up; the A&R men from every company in the country – Ahmet Ertegun at Atlantic, Aladdin in California, the Bihari brothers, Chess out of Chicago – come to me for advice.

So finally, I said, 'If I'm such an authority I'll go into the production end of the business myself.' I didn't know anything about manufacturing or distribution but music has always been a way of life for me so I just took a chance. I gathered what little information I could get and I went into the studio and started producing doo-wop groups. We were just at the beginning of the doo-wop period. There were a couple of groups out at that time – The Orioles and The Ravens. The Ravens were a jump type rhythm and blues group and The Orioles were a sentimental kind of a thing. They were the forerunner of the doo-wops.

I got some groups together. We didn't have any place to rehearse so what I did was close the record store an hour early at 11 and lock the doors and rehearse right inside. The first group I recorded was The Mellow Moods – a standard tune, 'Where Are You Now That I Need You'. I started to get very good success immediately. Once you start going everybody starts to run to you so then followed The Vocaleers, The Scarlets, The Teenchords. Altogether I introduced about 13 or 14 groups in that category.

Later on, Bobby produced hits by The Channels ('The Closer You Are') and The Charts ('Deserie'). In the bible of the doo-wop era, *They All Sang On the Corner*, Philip Groia describes how The Charts got themselves booed off stage at The Apollo Theatre amateur night 'for singing what the audience believed was a "weird" song. "Deserie" was a drag as it "wah-wahed" along with no channel [bridge] . . . They sang it right through the booing, onto the Everlast label and into three and a half million copies of the novel recording. No more hanging around corners anymore.' Unfortunately, as Groia points out, The Charts were too young to keep control of their success. They sold the rights of 'Deserie' to a photographer and after four more records for Bobby Robinson they vanished. The parallels with the rap scene are clear. Having lived and worked in the middle of both phenomena, Bobby draws the comparison:

Doo-wop originally started out as the black teenage expression of the '50s and rap emerged as the black teenage ghetto expression of the '70s. Same identical thing that started it – the doo-wop groups down the street, in hallways, in alleys and on the corner. They'd gather anywhere and, you know, doo wop doo wah da da da da. You'd hear it everywhere. So the same thing started with rap groups around '76 or so. All of a sudden, everywhere you turned you'd hear kids rapping. In the summertime, they'd have these little parties in the park. They used to go out and play at night and kids would be out there dancing. All of a sudden, all you could hear was, hip hop hit the top don't stop. It's kids – to a great extent mixed-up and confused – reaching out to express themselves. They were forcefully

BOBBY ROBINSON'S RECORD STORE, 125TH STREET

BOBBY'S
HAPPY HOUSE
RECORDS
Tapes & Accessories
301
RECORDS

trying to express themselves and they made up in fantasy what they missed in reality. The older guys who created doo-wop – it was a little different. They weren't so aggressive and volatile.

From doo-wop Robinson moved into rhythm and blues with Wilbert Harrison's 'Kansas City' ('after that it was a whole new ball game'), Buster Brown, Elmore James and Lightning Hopkins. Through the '50s he had formed a number of labels starting with Red Robin, then Whirlin' Disc followed by Fury ('I was pretty furious at some of the things that had happened with the Whirlin' Disc setup so I formed Fury as a label'), Fire and then, in 1963, Enjoy. The first record on Enjoy was the driving tenor-saxophone instrumental 'Soul Twist' by King Curtis, one of the major black instru-

THE CLOSER YOU ARE: THE CHANNELS
Photo: courtesy of Charlie Gillett

BOBBY ROBINSON AT HOME

mentalists to span the eras of '50s and '60s jazz and R&B through to '70s soul. Curtis, who died a violent death in 1971, was one of the artists who benefited from Bobby Robinson's ear for the commercial. After a brief period of success on Enjoy, King Curtis decided that greater rewards lay elsewhere and Bobby Robinson granted him a release from his contract to move to Capitol Records. This was a pattern that was to reassert itself in the '70s with most of the rap groups which recorded for Enjoy.

During the 1960s Bobby reactivated the Everlast label (previously run by his brother Danny) and had a million seller with Les Cooper's dance-craze disc 'Wiggle Wobble'. Successes became thinner on the ground and the operation ran into what he describes as a 'quagmire'. With the retail store still doing business he became a $100-a-day consultant for Pickwick International, a huge budget record company in Long Island, packaging black music records in a series called Soul Parade. He also made many lease deals for his back catalogue, which he now regrets. Like many older producers and artists, disco was a music which had little appeal for him:

> I'll tell you very frankly, I didn't have too high a regard for disco because what it was to me was like taking good-age Scotch and pouring it two-thirds with water. When I've got to sit down and produce music and count how many beats goes to a minute to hell with it. Black music is like a sixth-sense thing. You've got to feel it. I don't care how many beats it is. When they would take one line and say it over 130 times and that was a song – that really bugged me. It was a craze that caught on. The whole world was dance crazy. A lot of it was good but to me it just didn't have the substance that I thought music should have.

As disco began to wane as a fad Robinson felt that the time was right for him to release records again, and the charting of 'Rapper's Delight' pushed him into searching out some MC groups for himself. His scouts reported back to him from the deepest Bronx:

> There's a group called The Funky Four that have got a girl rapping with them called Sha Rock. That's a novelty 'cos she's the only girl out there. So I got that group first. We rehearsed in a garage – you press a button and the doors slide up – the guy backed his car into the street. We set the band up, the drums and guitar and everything; it was cold. It was mid-October and it was kind of chilly, so we let the gates down and we rehearsed. The Funky Four record took right off – called 'Rappin and Rockin the House'.

Released in 1979, the rhythm track for 'Rappin and Rockin' the House' was a version of Cheryl Lynn's debut, 'Got To Be Real', a single which had topped the R&B charts in January of that year. The drummer and bandleader on the session was Pumpkin, a young multi-instrumentalist who had started out playing jazz in high school and worked with a number of jazz fusion groups, including Triad, playing drums, bass and synthesiser. Funky Four's DJ Breakout had remembered Pumpkin always playing in a garage and recommended him to Bobby Robinson for their first (and only) Enjoy session. Clocking in at a length of 16 minutes, the record is a marathon to top 'Rapper's Delight'. Apart from a spectacular drum break by Pumpkin, the entire length is given over to rapping.

In the rush to get rap onto disc the most logical way to transfer live throwdowns onto tape was to take the favourite instrumental B sides that were being used by MC crews at the time, re-record them in their simplest form (guitar, bass and drums playing the chords and rhythmic structure), then overlay the rapping. The raps started about eight bars in and could usually be heard fading into the distance on the run-out groove. 'Rappin and Rockin the House' suffers from its lack of contrast but the feel is more innocent and the vocal interplay more dynamic than the Sugarhill debut, making it the more likeable release. Funky Four Plus One More were Lil Rodney Cee, KK Rockwell, Sha Rock, Keith Keith and Jazzy Jeff with DJ Breakout. KK Rockwell sketches in their history: ' I got started with Breakout. About seven or eight years ago there was just me and DJ Breakout. He got a partner, then along came Keith Keith, then Sha Rock, then we put Rahiem with us. He left us for Grandmaster Flash and that's when Rodney and Jeff joined with us and we turned to the Funky Four Plus One More'.

Their first experience as recording artists fell short of their expectations, although there seem to be no hard feelings directed at Enjoy. Rodney explains their disappointment:

> We were young at the time. When we signed the contract we were 16 and 17. Nobody was older than 17 in the group. We signed with Enjoy and it didn't turn out the way we expected it. All I knew, this guy came to me, he wanted to make a record and he told me I'm gonna be rich. That's what I expected. I expected to be rich for making a record and it didn't materialise. We made a nice little bit of money – it wasn't all that bad. We did a couple of shows. We went down south where it didn't turn out right because rap was new across the country. Right here in New York it was well accepted so we could play here and make crazy money.

It is hardly surprising that Funky Four's first release was so long (the longest single ever made?). For their live shows they were publicising themselves by handing out flyers and then performing from midnight to three or four in the morning, rapping straight through. Their dance routines were inspired by The Temptations. Ted Fox, in his book *Showtime At the Apollo*, talks about The Temptations' influence and the Apollo's effect on the Motown acts' stagecraft:

> What really ignited the Motown revues at the Apollo was the slick sophisticated choreography of the great male groups like The Four Tops and especially The

SLICK, SOPHISTICATED CHOREOGRAPHY: THE TEMPTATIONS *Photo: courtesy of Charlie Gillett*

Temptations. 'The Temps were known for that,' said Gladys Knight, 'and the Apollo Theatre perpetuated that style because it became popular with the audiences there, and they just ate it up.' Gladys Knight and the Pips had been on the scene professionally for ten years before the Motown revues began, but didn't join the Motown caravan until the mid-sixties. The Pips' dancing ability, fine-tuned by Honi Coles' partner, Cholly Atkins, was a tremendous influence on The Temptations.

The big attraction of The Temptations for The Funky Four was their professionalism. Though rap was relatively amateur it was fiercely competitive, and the group were aware that an entertaining stage show would give them an edge over the MCs who simply stood and ran their mouths. The dance steps were combined with raps to make little routines, some of them based on TV theme tunes like 'Gilligans Island'.

Bobby Robinson's scouts initially recommended two groups – The Funky Four Plus One More and Grandmaster Flash and the Furious Five. Flash remembers with some amusement the time Bobby came to see them play:

> When that record ['Rapper's Delight'] came out, little carry-your-records-in-a-trunk producers were coming out of the woodwork looking for any group that could do this. So I said to myself, I know my fans' age range is between 15 and 21. There was this little *old* man in the back – he was too old to be partying. Either he was in there looking for his daughter or son or he was the fucking cops. My manager went up to him after – could he help him? So he says, 'Why sure, I want to speak to these guys. I'm interested in cutting a record with them.' His name was Bobby Robinson.

The record was 'Superrappin''. Around the time of its release another 12-inch single appeared by a group calling themselves The Younger Generation. On Brass Records, it was called 'We Rock More Mellow' and was produced by Terry Lewis. This group was also the Furious Five – Melle Mel, Cowboy, Rahiem, Mr Ness and Kid Creole – under an assumed name. Considering the brief time lag between the two records, the differences are striking. The backing track for the Younger Generation tune is a leaden disco thumper with a shaky four-on-the-floor bass drum, and the rapping is a strictly follow-my-leader effort with the MCs sounding like the session was beginning to depress them. In contrast, 'Superrappin'' has the kind of pumping rhythm that characterised rap in its early days on disc – a brisk 114 bpm with the bass drum playing syncopations that hadn't been heard in dance music for some years.

The Furious Five's rapping style was a revelation. Lines were divided up between individuals and cut in with unison ensembles and solos which highlighted the different vocal qualities and styles. They also duplicated Flash's spin-backs and quick cuts, repeating syllables as if the stylus was dropping back into the same groove – 'That Flash was on the beat box going . . . an . . . an . . . an . . . an . . . sha-na-na'.

The group had been asked to make a record some years previously but Flash was reluctant, thinking that a used beat and some talking was no competition for the plush orchestral sound that was predominant during that period. He has reservations about 'Superrappin'':

> I enjoyed 'Superrappin'' to a point and then again I didn't. It could have been done better 'cos if you listen the tempo speeds up after a while. The band goes out of wack a little bit. After a while we

were waiting to hear 'Superrappin' ' on the radio because this other rap record, The Sugarhill Gang, they were on the air. What power do Sugarhill have to get something on the radio like *that* and we can't get *ours* on it? Ours sounds better than theirs. Bobby didn't really have the push to get us out there. We got kinda angry with him and we went to the Hill.

Bobby Robinson had suffered, in fact, from his long lay-off from the business:

I'm off and running with Enjoy and with two smash hit records. I really wasn't organised on a national basis because I'd been out of it for a while. I could have had much bigger records had I really been geared. I operated most of the eastern seaboard from here to Florida. I spread a little bit west but I wasn't really geared with the national distribution linkage. I found myself caught up in it. I thought it was a fad that will last a little while and blow over and I'll get into my other thing. I had no idea it would be as long drawn-out as it has been.

The radio stations were all very touchy but I'll tell you the truth – I didn't miss it because with the rap records, luckily for a lot of small companies who had trouble with airplay and credibility, the rap thing was like wildfire without the radio. You see, you cover all the discos and disco pools and mobile jocks – everybody that's got a mike in their hand, give 'em records. And stores – in-store play – put 'em on the speakers outside in the street and the kids would line up. So I broke the records wide open without the air.

Although Bobby was fast off the mark, the time it took him to realise what was going on cost him another first. After Flash and the Five he paired The Treacherous Three with Spoonie Gee. One side was the tongue-twisting 'The New Rap Language', a rap with a nod to Mary Poppins which set a new style of quickfire rhyming against a 112 bpm beat with a slowish feel. On drums was Pumpkin, and featured on congas was Pooche Costello, Spoonie Gee's brother (currently answering the phone at Enjoy Records). The other side was 'Love Rap', a solo rap by Spoonie Gee, with just voice, drums and congas. One of the very few

LOVE RAP: SPOONIE GEE AT DANCETERIA

commercially released raps with only beats for backing, it has been a consistently big seller for Bobby right up until the present. He confesses how he missed out once again:

> Spoonie was raised right here in this house. Pooche Costello, the conga player, that's Spoonie Gee's brother. Their mother was my wife's baby sister and they lived down the hall – same floor, last apartment. She died suddenly and Spoonie was 12, Pooche was about 14, and my wife took them in and gave them that back room there.
>
> He did his first rapping right in this room – wearing out my records! He'd sit over in that corner day after day. He'd play my records. My wife used to run him out of here sometimes. She'd say, 'Get out of here with that noise. All day long that yap-yap-yap.' He put together that very first thing that he did in this room to my music but I was so involved at the time. I had three or four things going on. This guy, Peter Brown, he was in my record store one night and he said, 'I'd like to cut a rap record', and somebody says, 'Spoonie can rap'.

As a result of this scene from an M.G.M. musical, Spoonie Gee cut 'Spoonin' Rap' on Sounds of New York USA, one of Peter Brown's bewilderingly full hand of labels. It also appeared on an album on Queen Constance Records called *The Big Break Rapper Party* and was remixed and re-released in 1984 on Heavenly Star. For Brown (not the Peter Brown who recorded 'Do Ya Wanna Get Funky With Me'), record production was a hustle among hustles. His other labels included Golden Flamingo and Land of Hits, the records frequently classics of low-budget incompetence. If the label said 33 it was 45; singers sang and rappers rapped out of time; drummers lost the beat, and the sound was as garage as they come. A number of these releases had appeal as golden turkeys, but from amidst the general mass of garbage Spoonie Gee shone through as a real talent.

Spoonie is currently working as a supervisor in a rehabilitation centre for the mentally disabled where he is known by his real name of Gabe Jackson (his nickname came from his fondness for eating with a spoon when he was a small boy). 'Spoonin' Rap' was the first release on a journey through three different labels before his current signing at Aaron Fuchs's Tuff City Records. He already sounds self-assured, fluently rolling out the seduction routine that has become his trademark over a slinky backing track of bass and drums, some flexatone and whistles. With his tall tales, sexual boasting and badman stories, Spoonie is closest to the mythical Jody, the woman stealer and death dealer. However regrettable outsiders might find the sexism of his songs, they are part of a line in black oral literature and song which extends at its furthest limit to Spoonie's favourite form of music, the romantic soul ballad: 'I'm into all types of music but I like the type of music I can lay back to and listen. I like old records, old and new, but I like slow ballads. I'll take slow music over fast music any day. I like Marvin Gaye, Nat King Cole, Brook Benton. I like, God bless the dead, Jackie

Wilson. I even liked Elvis. I can't forget Barry White'.

If Spoonie identifies with the balladeers, Kurtis Blow sees himself as being somewhere between Chic and James Brown. The sound of 1979 was rappers splashing into wax, and Kurtis leaped with the leaders. His 'Christmas Rapping' appeared on Mercury at the end of the year. The bass line was a distant cousin to 'Good Times'; the guitarists obviously knew a thing or two about Nile Rodgers and Jimmy Nolan (the late great guitar chair with the JBs), there was even an echo of Junior Wells's 'Messing With the Kid', not to mention a key change and a very funky piano player, Denzil Miller. Rap on record had come a long way in a few months.

Kurtis was another soloist with Harlem origins, a mobile jock playing James Brown records in Queens who was struck by DJ Hollywood's popularity at the 371 Club in the Bronx. For a brief period he worked with Grandmaster Flash, and in summer '79 was spotted at The Hotel Diplomat by his producers, JB Moore and Robert Ford Jr, and offered a deal.

Rap was a performance medium. It was a throwback to the days when musicians made singles which approximated to their live show, albums were hastily-thrown-together hotch potches of hits with filler, and overdubbing was virtually unheard of. Signing to Mercury, with its Polygram distribution, and working with a team of lyricists which included Moore and Ford as well as his manager, Russell Simmons, Kurtis was the first to combine hip hop with a '70s concept of production and marketing. In 1980 he released an album which obviously attempted to cross him over to a broader audience. The songs took basic b boy rhymes and moulded them into themes with a humorous or moral twist. There was even a rock song – Bachman Turner Overdrive's 'Takin' Care of Business' – and a ridiculous ballad with Kurtis revealing a surprisingly frail voice.

The big track was 'The Breaks', a 1980 hit which gave rap some of the tautness of a comedy routine (partly through being inspired by Eddie Lawrence, a white comic). Thanks to Roddy Hui's engineering, the track had a terrific clarity. The bass and drums were used as a foundation, reggae style, for a clever arrangement of the other instruments, in particular the fierce percussion breaks traded off between Jamie Delgado's timbales and Jimmy Bralower's tom toms. Kurtis Blow may not have been 100 per cent proof Bronx hip hop, but his early records helped set the style in post-disco dance music.

One of the constants of rap is its machismo. On the front cover of his first album Kurtis is bare-chested, hung with gold chains showing off his pectorals. The look is 'tough' and the eyes are sincere but steady. Considering the rich heritage of female vocalists in black music it is surprising that women rappers have not had greater success. In the early days of hip hop Grandmaster Flash remembers there being more female crews than male. Of the few fixed groups in those days one was entirely female – The Mercedes Ladies (Zena Z, Debbie D, Eva Deff and Sherry Sheryl, with RC and Baby D as DJs). Rodney and

Kevin of Double Trouble recall their rise and fall: 'They were from the Bronx. But they came in and went out fast,' says Rodney. Kevin elaborates: 'Slowly but surely their name was getting out there. People was getting to know them but they gave up. They even played with us one time and it was packed. Right there, that's a lot of publicity for them. They should have stayed with it. The girl DJ was good – she definitely should have stayed with it. Sha Rock stuck with it and she mastered it.'

Since rapping has strong roots in the predominantly male activities of toasts and dozens, it is not surprising that men see it as the musical equivalent of a sport like baseball. They are prepared to accept that women can do it but see the competitive element as the final deterrent. Flash has a paternalistic attitude to it:

> There was the Mercedes Ladies, Sha Rock, Lisa Lee – there was quite a few, but a lot of them gave up. See, what it is in this highly competitive sort of entertainment there's very few females I see made it. I even tried to show some of them the proper way of going about it. I've seen one DJ – she was pretty good. She thought she was as good as me. That's good to have that type of spirit. She was good but she just stopped. Now she's on West End Records – Baby D, D'bora. She was pretty good back in that day. She was the DJ for the Mercedes Ladies, a whole female crew, and that's what they need right now. I'm talking about a real good DJ and some good MCs that really know how to shake it and

entertain the crowd. They'd make money. They'd make a killing right now 'cos what's happening right now is everything is becoming repetitious.

Women associated with the scene, on the other hand, feel that men tend to disapprove of their standing in front of a crowd bragging and boasting. But in some cases they go along with the men: shouting about yourself might be all right when you're young but as you get older it's 'unladylike'. In the first few years of recording a high proportion of raps featured girls – Funky Four Plus One More, Lady D on Reflection Records, The CC Crew on Golden Flamingo, Naomi Peterson on Heavenly Star, Cosmic Force and Paulette and Tanya Winley on Winley Records, Philadelphia DJ Lady B on Tec Records and Sequence on Sugarhill.

At Danceteria on West 21st the diminutive duo Double Trouble and dancers Electric Force are hosting a 'graffiti wedding celebration' in honour of Rodney's marriage to Angie B of Sequence. At the end of the show Angie B and Cheryl the Pearl come out to perform a song, handing out copies of their album and explaining that their third member, Blondie, is in Los Angeles right now. Although their voices don't yet have the emotional depth of a gospel group like the Barrett Sisters, they certainly look the part. Sequence were originally a singing group from Columbia, South Carolina, whose break came when they went to a Sugarhill Gang concert in the

ARM WRESTLING AT THE FUNHOUSE

summer of 1979. One of the Gang's road managers took a liking to Angie B but found himself having to listen to the whole group giving an impromptu performance of a song they had written called 'Funk You Up'. Probably feeling out of his depth, he took them backstage to meet Sylvia Robinson, who auditioned them then and there and within three weeks had sent them plane tickets and recorded their tune.

'Funk You Up' is one of the classic boasting raps, with Blondie (not the Debbie Harry version) telling the boys in the house not to ring her bell if they can't fulfil her needs. Culture heroes like Fred Astaire and Ginger Rogers, Fred Flintstone and Yogi Bear are invoked, and the Sugarhill houseband sound extremely powerful, with Doug Wimbish's visceral bass tangling with the voices.

On all of the early rap records featuring women, the women rap as well as the men – in some cases far better. 'Vicious Rap' by Sweet Tee, in particular, is a refreshing blast of old-style R&B. The drummer plays with the snares off, there's an organ stabbing away underneath the guitar (probably played by Dave 'Baby' Cortez) and Sweet Tee raps out a tough story of false arrest. The sound may be boxy and lacking in production, and the tempo speeds up, but the excitement is there.

Sweet Tee, who also raps with her sister on 'Rhymin and Rappin' had her records produced by her mother, Ann Winley, and released by her father, Paul Winley. This family enterprise can be found on 125th Street. If you look up you see a smart logo and a painted sign saying PAUL WINLEY RECORDS INC. Look down and you see a

SEQUENCE AT DANCETERIA

different picture. Winley Records has obviously seen better days. The storefront has an unkempt display of record sleeves – Afrika Bambaataa, Malcolm X, Martin Luther King, Gloria Lynne – and inside are the signs of having worked on the far edges of an already marginalised field of music. Despite his notorious reputation among certain sectors of the New York record business, Paul Winley is a friendly and obliging man with a resigned, philosophical attitude to the consequences of cutting corners in matters of copyright. He describes his starting point in music:

> I started in the business from writing songs. My brother had a group called the Clovers and I started writing songs for them in Washington. They used to come to New York to record for Atlantic – and I used to come up with them. I met Ahmet Ertegun and all of us became very good friends. Everybody at Atlantic at that time was like family so after moving here from Washington in '52–'53 I just stayed. I used to spend a lot of time at Atlantic. They had artists like Ray Charles, Ruth Brown, Joe Turner – I remember writing songs for Ruth Brown and Joe Turner.
>
> From Atlantic I hit the street and started writing around the Brill Building which was 1619. In the old days that's where all the songwriters and all the

PAUL WINLEY

PAUL WINLEY RECORDS, 125TH STREET

black entertainers would meet – on Broadway, 49th and Broadway, which is now Colony Records. We would congregate round there, write songs and shoot the breeze. I did that for a number of years, then in 1956 I started my own record company. A lot of publishers to survive at that time went into starting their own record companies. In order for a songwriter to give a publisher a song he had to damn near have a record. There was a group of songwriters. There was about six or seven of us – there was a feller named Otis Blackwell who wrote for Elvis. There was a feller named Winfield Scat who wrote 'Tweedle Dee'. There was a feller we considered our teacher – his name is Jesse Stone but they called him Charles Calhoun. He wrote 'Shake Rattle and Roll', 'Money Honey', a lot of songs. He was the real backbone of the songwriters.

Winley had a songwriting partnership with Davey Clowney, later known as Dave 'Baby' Cortez, and the two of them started recording doo-wop groups:

First thing I recorded was by 'Baby' Cortez, then a feller named Little Anthony. He had a group called the Duponts – we recorded them. Nothing happened too much and then we recorded The Paragons. A friend of mine wanted me to hear these kids out in Brooklyn and they were real hoodlums, real zip-gun street-warring hoodlums, you know, but at the time I was young and crazy myself so it didn't make any difference. We got together and listened to them and the guy that sang lead had a song called 'Florence' and they could never sing the damn thing twice in the same way. We finally got 'em into the studio and we recorded 'Florence', and there was another group from the east side here called The Jesters who recorded, so I had two good groups. Then another group came along, with a good song, called The Collegians – they made a record called 'Zoom Zoom Zoom' for me. We had a lot of good things here and there in the '50s, and then in the '60s we recorded The Jesters who rearranged their group and re-recorded a thing called 'The Wind'.

With Moms Mabley for his godmother and other comics like Nipsey Russell, Pigmeat Markham and Flip Wilson as friends, Paul was very aware that rap was just another chapter in a rich tradition of black vocal artistry:

Rapping goes back. Rapping is an old thing. Like a lot of black singers couldn't sing but they could talk. My brother, the one who used to be with The Clovers, is singing now with a group called The Inkspots – the original management group of The Inkspots. If you go back to that era, the part my brother does is the bass 'cos he was bass with The Clovers, so now he talks. James Brown did rapping, Isaac Hayes did rapping, Millie Jackson did rapping – rapping is nothing new.

Apart from recording his own family in the late '70s, Winley also put down tracks by two of Afrika Bambaataa's MC crews, Cosmic Force and Soul Sonic Force. 'Zulu Nation Throwdown' by Cosmic Force was released in 1980. Neither Winley nor Bambaataa are too happy about the record, and Bambaataa doesn't bother to hide his contempt for the company:

> A wack company. It was jive. He put out a record called Afrika Bambaataa's 'Death Mix'. That is a tape like – suppose she came to my party and made a tape and she made a copy for you and you made a copy for me and I took the tape and gave it to him and he put it on record. It sounds like doo doo! He had the nerve to put on the back, 'I'm sorry for the first two records I did with you. You my friend' and all that. It was really a bootleg type of mess. We didn't get any money for the first record. The first two he made was ugly anyway. I went to him saying I could make his company move. I had ideas but he didn't pay us no mind.
>
> 'Zulu Nation Throwdown, Part One' helped us to get downtown. A lot of the new-wave people liked it. It surprised me 'cos I couldn't stand it until I heard it on the Ritz system. I started coming to clubs and they were playing it a lot and I started liking it. Then we made Part Two with Soul Sonic Force which never went nowhere. This company was just terrible.

Despite Bambaataa's dislike of Winley Records, it was the only company prepared to release his material in the early days. He had been working on a version of Sly Stone's 'Sing a Simple Song' in the Sugarhill Studios with George Kerr (an intriguing project which came to nothing), but what he was hearing about Sylvia Robinson was anything but encouraging. Sending a tape to Enjoy proved fruitless, so Winley was the next stop.

The Cosmic Force 12-inch is high on charm, with a Chitty Chitty Bang Bang throwaway and some strong lines in a James Brown mould from Lisa Lee:

> *Rock it to the sounds that make you dance*
> *Make the ants crawl in your pants*
> *Put you in a music trance.*

In his sleeve notes for *The Best of Winley Records* on Relic Records, Donn Fileti's analysis of Winley's doo-wop approach in relation to bigger companies could just as easily apply to the '70s:

> There's a kind of down-to-earth, almost amateurish quality to the records that Winley produced in the late '50s which made them almost impossible to duplicate; his sound could only have come from an imaginative independent operator – the major labels thought the group sound was easy to copy but their abject failure with New York-type vocal groups was partly in trying to employ expensive production values for street-corner harmonizers, which Winley disdained (and could not afford). The Paul Winley sound is unique, and could only have come out of New York City.

Winley describes his entry into the rap market:

> In the '70s when the rapping started I put out some records called *Super Disco Brakes* and the kids would use certain breaks in these records to rap. I recorded my two daughters. One of my daughters was a rap fanatic. Every time I looked at her she had her head in her notebook. I said, 'Well, how much homework you got? You really must love school!' But she was actually writing rhymes. That's Tanya. Paulette wasn't into that – she was more into singing.
>
> A couple of dealers who used to buy these records from me said, 'Hey Paul, why don't you make one rap record because these kids – *anything* – if you put out something with the raps it'll go.' I said, 'But every kid on the block is rapping.' They said, 'But they just want to hear it on record.' That's the reason I hesitated. I would have recorded rap before Sugarhill was even thought of – long before Bobby Robinson cut rap – because these guys didn't know what was going on. I was in the street selling my break records so I was very familiar. I knew they were buying the records to do the raps off.

Given the extraordinary subsequent influence of hip hop all over the world – scratch mix seminars in Japan, rap radio in Holland, breakdance fever in Germany, smurf madness in France, rap clubs and crews in Britain – the reticence of rappers and label owners to record is puzzling. In many cases there was a resignation to being shut off from the mainstream – physically, politically, culturally – at a time when much black music had crossed over to a non-black audience. In the middle '70s an enormous amount of black music was achieving sales in the international mass market. Although all of it derived from strands of the black music tradition, the degree of success tended to be proportional to the absence of rawness, and the phrase 'too black for the charts' became common music-business jargon.

With Sugarhill proving that there was a new market for streetcorner sounds, the old-time entrepreneurs dusted off the ancient contracts and moved in. Jack Taylor, from Rojac Records, who in the '60s had recorded Big Maybelle records like 'Don't Pass Me By', recorded pioneer MC Starski, and Danny Robinson, Bobby Robinson's brother, briefly revived his Holiday label (home of The Bop Chords in 1956) for The Nice and Nasty Three's 'The Ultimate Rap' in 1980. The early records are confusing, partly because they transferred a sound-system-based music onto disc and partly because some of the artists were recorded not so much for their talent but because they happened to hang out down the block from the record company. Although most hip-hop innovators had found their way onto disc by 1980, it was initially difficult for a casual listener to tell who were the opportunists and who were the originals. It may not all have been good but it was definitely fresh.

"THUNDER ON THURSDAY"
STARRING
Negril·2nd ave.
11th & 12th st
INGREDIBLE "WHIZ KID" INGREDIBLE
MC Rammell Zee
D J KOOL HERC
MC Prince $hockdell
Futura -2000's- Futura
"SprayGrafix"
N.Y.C.
SYMPHONIC B·BOYS MIXX
maxamillion·rockin' shamel
ROCK ON!
FEB.25,1982·11PM·DAMAGE:
5
Sure Shot Party Crew 4u
LEE 163D! & SKI 168
Kool Lady Blue Too!

8. Version to version

One of the first signs that the early flurry of rap recordings had registered an impact outside of its own back yard was the release of a cover version of 'Rapper's Delight' on Joe Gibbs's reggae label in 1979. 'Rapper's Delight' and 'Rocker's Choice' by Xanadu and Sweet Lady is rapped, quasi-Bronx style, on one side, and toasted, Jamaican style, on the other. Given the Caribbean background of three of the prime movers in hip hop (Kool DJ Herc, Afrika Bambaataa and Grandmaster Flash), the similar foundation of rap and reggae in sound systems and radio DJs, and the number of Bronx, Harlem and Brooklyn residents with roots in the West Indies, it is surprising that there were not more crossovers of this type. According to Jervis Anderson's book, *Harlem: The Great Black Way*: 'In the nineteen-thirties, more than twenty per cent of Harlem's black population were people from the West Indies.' Tempting as it might be to imagine that hip hop emerged simply through the influence of Jamaican toasters like U Roy and Big Youth, it was, in fact, more subtle than that. Most rappers will tell you that they either disliked reggae or were only vaguely aware of it in the early and middle '70s. Although Jamaican-run record companies like Clocktower (now defunct after the killing of label boss Brad Osbourne), Bullwackies and Clappers exist in New York, there have been remarkably few musical collaborations between reggae and funk.

In the same way in which salsa has been plundered but rarely met on its own terms, reggae has been an influence on isolated records ('Rock the House' by Pressure Drop on Tommy Boy or Sugarhill's remake of 'Love Is Strange' by The Word) or on studio techniques. Dub mixes began to appear in 1982, particularly from The Peech Boys, François Kervorkian's mixes of Forrrce and D Train, and Nick Martinelli and David Todd's mixes of Raw Silk and Brenda Taylor.

With sound systems at their heart, reggae and rap share a partial reliance on previously recorded rhythms. In all the stories of pre-disc hip hop the only musicians are the ones on the DJ's records. The rock or soul impulse to form a band, rehearse and play gigs was supplanted by the magic attraction of the twin turntables. Ask the majority of DJs and MCs if they play an instrument and they'll probably offer 'beat box' as a reply. This is changing gradually as groups develop their ideas in recording studios, but in its basic form hip hop has stayed true to its house-party origins.

The time it took for record companies to move in on hip hop in New York allowed a huge build-up of innovative techniques and quirky styles which then had to be translated into a playable instrumental form and adapted for mass public consumption.

Though many of the rap/scratch records that have been released since 1979 sound unique, they are mostly polished versions of the kind of thing every kid on the block was doing. This is particularly true of Malcolm McLaren 'Buffalo Gals' single and its follow ups, the *Duck Rock* album and other related projects like Art of Noise. All of them were crucial in bringing acceptance of hip-hop attitudes to a very wide audience (and, to be fair, had an influence back into hip hop). *Duck Rock* was a hi-tech version of the kind of inspired musical collisions that were commonplace at the time when McLaren's attention was focused on scandalising the world with The Sex Pistols.

In the who-dares-wins delirium of the house parties, Bambaataa mixed up calypso, European and Japanese electronic music, Beethoven's Fifth Symphony and rock groups like Mountain; Kool DJ Herc spun The Doobie Brothers back-to-back with the Isley Brothers; Grandmaster Flash overlayed speech records and sound effects with The Last Poets; Symphonic B Boys Mixx cut up classical music on five turntables, and a multitude of unknowns unleashed turntable wizardry with their feet, heads, noses, teeth and tongues. In a crazy new sport of disc jockey acrobatics, musical experiment and virtuosity were being combined with showmanship. Earlier in black music history the same potent spirit had compelled Lionel Hampton to leap onto his drums, Big Jay McNeely to play screaming saxophone lying on the stage and the guitar aces – T Bone Walker, Earl Hooker, Johnny Guitar Watson and Jimi Hendrix – to pick the strings with their teeth or behind their heads.

A few small groups of studio musicians were given the job of converting all this sound-system mayhem and verbal wildstyle into marketable recordings. The All Platinum set-up in Englewood had maintained two studios as well as a house band called Wood, Brass and Steel, all of which transferred to Sugarhill with the incorporation of the new company. Keith LeBlanc, a white drummer, bassist Doug Wimbish and guitarist Bernard Alexander formed the early nucleus of the Sugarhill band, along with a horn section called Chops. Later additions included guitarist Skip MacDonald, percussionist Ed Fletcher (Duke Bootee of 'The Message' and 'Survival' fame) and keyboardists Gary Henry, Duane Mitchell, Reggie Griffen and Clifton 'Jiggs' Chase. Jiggs, whose dues include the organ chair in flautist Joe Thomas's '60s soul jazz group (comping behind the soloists on Hammond organ), has also been the arranger on most of Sugarhill's rap output as well as mixing tracks with engineer Steve Jerome. The biggest credit is generally given to Sylvia Robinson as producer and co-writer, though some Sugarhill artists (mostly those who have fled the company) question the extent of her actual contribution. What all give her credit for is her ability to spot records with strong, usable rhythms for potential raps.

When Flash and The Furious Five moved from Enjoy to Sugarhill, signing their contract on the bonnet of a car, Sylvia offered them a backing track for their first release, a single called 'Freedom'. Flash explains the circumstances:

> What was hot from the b boy scene was this record called 'Get Up and Dance' by this group called Freedom, on TK Records. This was what all the DJs were cutting – disco DJs and b boys DJs. What she did is she took it and recut it,

reconstructed it herself, and she had it on 24-track tape in the studio, so when I met Sylvia Robinson, me and Raheim, she was saying she could get us on that record if we signed.

Funky Four Plus One More also moved from Enjoy to Sugarhill, losing the last word from their name somewhere in the Hudson River but still clutching their idea for a rhythm track. Their debut for the new label was 'That's the Joint', a slower re-arranged version of 'Rappin' and Rockin' the House', with LeBlanc's bass drum and Wimbish's bass kicking at the front of the mix. Although 'Freedom' was credited to its original writers, 'That's the Joint' was given to Funky Four, Sylvia and Jiggs. The general rule among companies was to ignore copyright on the original rhythm until there was trouble. 'Rapper's Delight', for example, was initially credited to The Sugarhill Gang and Sylvia, but later pressings gave total authorship to Chic's Bernard Edwards and Nile Rodgers, the writers of 'Good Times'.

Edwards and Rodgers have seen 'Good Times' reappear on numerous occasions in various guises. An Atlanta disc jockey named Vaughan Mason released a floor-shaking riff called 'Bounce, Rock, Skate, Roll' on Brunswick in 1979 which was clearly based on 'Good Times'. Like an omen of things to come, it was the funk equivalent of heavy metal – guitar, vocals and percussion all extraneous dressing on the demolition-derby bass at its immovable centre. Mason, who claimed authorship of this multi-imaged riff, then saw his track reappear on the launch release for a new label called Sound of New York (not to be confused with Peter Brown's Sound of New York, USA). It was used as a backing track for a rap called 'Rap, Bounce, Rockskate' by two young MCs called Jerry Miller and Eric Isles, working under the name Trickeration. Authorship this time went to the company's president and vice-president, Gene Griffen and Bill Scarborough respectively.

The big hit of 1980 was Queen's 'Another One Bites the Dust', a song which pushed the Chic riff a little bit further from its origins and gave mixers the opportunity to slip from one version to another. This culminated in Grandmaster Flash's challenge to the world, 'The Adventures of Grandmaster Flash On the Wheels Of Steel' (Sugarhill, 1981), a devastating collage of Queen, Chic, The Sugarhill Gang's '8th Wonder', The Furious Five's 'Birthday Party', Sequence and Spoonie Gee's 'Monster Jam' and Blondie's 'Rapture'. It also overlayed a Disney-sounding story, the source of which Flash is keeping a firm secret.

All of the tracks used by Flash for his in-studio cut-up tie together – 'Monster Jam', 'Birthday Party' and '8th Wonder' all share the distinctive Sugarhill band sound. 'Birthday Party' is a do-over of 'Freedom' with a bridge sounding suspiciously like McFadden and Whitehead's 'Ain't No Stopping Us Now', and 'Monster Jam' is yet another 'Good Times' derivation which links the Queen and Chic tracks. The Blondie song, their homage to hip hop, is used for its namecheck of Flash – the

Grandmaster drops the needle back on the beginning of 'Flash is fast' three times just to prove how fast he is.

The passage of years since the bombshell release of 'Adventures' makes it easier to hear the differences between Flash's techniques and those of the newer-mix DJs. His scratching, in particular, has a harsh and grainy quality and a terrific rhythmic drive. Comparing him with scratch DJs like Grandmixer D.ST or Whiz Kid is like comparing John Lee Hooker's guitar playing with B.B. King's. The instrument and the musical genre are the same but the individual approaches are a mile apart.

'Adventures On the Wheels of Steel' was the first record really to show that rap was something other than an offshoot of disco. Where other releases *translated* hip hop, 'Adventures' was as close as any record would ever come to *being* hip hop.

Alongside 'Good Times', one of the other big version rhythms was Taana Gardner's Heartbeat'. Rap had applied the brakes to disco's pace and taken off its frenetic edge. 'Heartbeat' more or less ground it to a halt. Introduced by a disturbingly unsteady heartbeat and claps like gunfire, 'Heartbeat' seems to hang on to its funereal rhythm like a cardiac-arrest victim clinging to life. On any other record it might have been a disastrous move but the tension and slowness in the rhythm worked with Taana Gardner's strange quivering voice to create a pervasive trance atmosphere that is intensely compelling. The record sold in enormous quantities for West End Records and established three volatile careers – those of Taana Gardner, Kenton Nix (producer and writer, and currently a boxing trainer) and Larry Levan (Paradise Garage DJ and producer for The Peech Boys). Dennis Weeden, who played guitar on the session, remembers its impact:

> 'Heartbeat' was one of my greatest experiences and I must say it sure was an inspiration because when I did that record I had no idea it was going to jump off like it did. When we were in the studio recording it I said to myself, 'Now come on – this is never gonna make it.' It was just that type of tune where it seemed like it was not gonna happen, and then the next thing I know they were playing it five, six or seven times a day, just rotating, rotating different mixes. Didn't it revolutionise the whole thing? It turned everything around.

Dennis also played on Sweet G's 'A Heartbeat Rap', which used the same heartbeat (still pumping) and clap tracks as the original. Other rap versions of the rhythm included 'Life On the Planet Earth' by Pee Wee Mel and Barry B on 12 Star Records and 'Feel the Heartbeat', an excellent Enjoy release by The Treacherous Three (Kool Moe Dee, Special K and L.A. Sunshine) who made their debut with Spoonie Gee.

For radio play, Taana Gardner's 'Heartbeat' is sometimes played back-to back with another Kenton Nix composition and production, Gwen McCrae's 'Funky Sensation' released on Atlantic in 1981. Again the rhythm and distinctive bass riff were ideal for MCs, and a version followed on Tom

Silverman's Tommy Boy Records, a fledgling label then sited on East 85th Street. 'Jazzy Sensation' was an important record in that it brought together Afrika Bambaataa and his MCs The Jazzy Five with two white disc jockeys who were to have a profound influence on dance music of all kinds in years to come – Arthur Baker, who produced the record, and Shep Pettibone, the mixer and arranger. Apart from the Winley release, various Bambaataa MCs had previously recorded as Cotton Candy on Tommy Boy, but this was the first record that did justice to their abilities – not to mention Bam's imaginative ideas.

'Jazzy Sensation' has three mixes, one with the Jazzy Five's rap, one by Kryptic Krew featuring Tina B, and one an instrumental, and all move away from the dominant Sugarhill/Enjoy sound, using unusual sounds like friction drums, car horns and electronic clave. Tina B's rap, and particularly the instrumental, with synthesiser revoicing over the original percussion track, suggested that the guitar, bass and drums trio might be on the way out. Of the two individuals responsible for the music track, Pettibone was a pioneer of the radio mastermixes heard on Kiss FM. Mastermixing was a parallel development to the b boys' cutting and scratching, a way of intercutting and juxtaposing records in a way that completely transformed them and collaged them into long sequences. After 'Jazzy Sensation' Pettibone moved towards the dub style as well as reviving classic disco sounds by singers like Loleatta Holloway for a permanently appreciative audience of club dancers. Arthur Baker, on the other hand, became a crucial figure on the rap scene.

SHAKEDOWN SOUND: ARTHUR BAKER

Baker began in music as a club disc jockey in Boston, playing Philadelphia soul. After a while he moved into record production:

> The first thing that I really did, I had every relative who would speak to me give me $1,000. I was in Boston – everything was a lot cheaper. I did like 10 cuts. I went in totally over my head. I didn't know what I was doing – I had strings and

horns and spent all this money. I didn't have enough to finish it so I hooked up with Tom Moulton and he offered me like $2,500 for seven songs, 10 songs, whatever the hell it was. I jumped at it 'cos that was a way to pay my debts. I didn't make any money but I at least paid my debts.

I did a few records for Emergency. 'Happy Days' by Northend and Michelle Wallace. I had all these records and I was doing a few more little things. When I did 'Happy Days' I moved down here for the summer. I started meeting new musicians and getting turned on to different things – the rap music. This was like summer '79. This guy Joe Bataan, who's like a salsa musician – we were going to do an album for London Records, co-producing, so the first thing we went in to do was a rap record, 'Rap-O-Clap-O'. He took me up to all these rap clubs and he said, these were the words, 'Someone's gonna make a million dollars on this rap music.' I just said, 'No way!' I liked it, but . . .

So we did 'Rap-O-Clap-O' but what happened was London Records went under and he took the tapes and I didn't know what happened to them. I moved back to Boston and then six months later the record came out. I got no credit on it. Marty Sheller ws the arranger but that record – there really wasn't much to it. All it was was a rip off of 'Got To Be Real' – Cheryl Lynn's record.

Joe Bataan is a musician like Jimmy Castor who embraces many different aspects of New York music. An ex-leader of Spanish Harlem gangs The Young Copasetics and The Dragons, he was one of the driving forces behind Latin soul in the '60s. His *Riot* album from 1969 is an exultant mix of bugalu, doo-wops like 'Daddy's Coming Home' and high-spirited R&B. Featuring his group The Latin Swingers ('from 98th to 110th Streets') and pupils from Taft High School, its mood spells out the positive side of the urban gangs. The sleevenotes say it all: 'P.S. The Riot is a song of joy and good feelings expressed thru music and not of violence.' The arranger on 'Rap-O-Clap-O', Marty Sheller, worked on another Latin rap, Tito Allen's 1980 'Salsa Rap' on Alegre which, along with the rapping on Bataan's *Mestizo* album, is about the extent of rap's penetration into the older-generation Latin music.

Arthur Baker tells how his introduction to rap led him to get more fully involved:

> I was aware of this stuff from when it first happened. Then I did another record called 'Can You Guess What Groove This Is' by a group called Glory. It was on Posse Records and it was one of the first medleys. It had 'Good Times' and all this stuff and it was done around the time of 'Rapper's Delight'. So I was into that but I didn't really get involved until I moved to New York. Then, two months later, I hooked up with Tom Silverman and we were gonna go in and do two rap records. I had no money so he was going to finance it. We were going to do 'Genius of Love' and 'Funky Sensation' – a rap on that. The night we went in we heard that four other people were doing 'Genius of Love', so we just did 'Funky Sensation'. So from there I hooked up with Bambaataa. We did 'Planet Rock'. I did 'Walking On Sunshine' and we started Streetwise Records.

Baker sees the versioning of other people's tunes as being a kind of jazz: 'The way I look at it, it's sort of like a jazz music. It's like rearranging. Like when John Coltrane does 'My Favourite Things' it doesn't sound like it's gonna sound if some lounge singer does it. They rearrange it and it comes out differently'. As Arthur suggests, there was a bandwagon-jumping attitude to using popular rhythm tracks. It was similar, in some ways, to the cover-version syndrome of the '50s and early '60s (not to mention the early '80s), though in contrast to the Pat Boone/Paul Young type of approach, rap versions usually threw a completely new light on the originals.

Interesting complications arose as white musicians moved out of rock and into funk. Blondie and Queen were both recycled by Grandmaster Flash in 'Adventures On the Wheels of Steel'. Flash and The Furious Five also used Tom Tom Club's 'Genius of Love' for 'It's Nasty', and Tom Tom Club, a Talking Heads spin-off, had their own rap hit, 'Wordy Rappinghood', in 1981. It was 'Genius of Love' which had everybody rushing into the studio to redo its bumpy, nursery-school funk. One of the most intriguing 'genius' records was Dr Jeckyl and Mr Hyde's 'Genius Rap' on Profile Records. Profile is a New York company which started out in May 1981 with an English record by Grace Kennedy. Their second release was a rap called 'Young Ladies' by Lonnie Love, who later drank the potion and turned into the Mr Hyde half of the 'Genius Rap' duo.

In the Profile offices somewhere near the top of a high-rise on West 57th, 26-year-old co-president Cory Robbins is explaining how 'Genius Rap' came to be made. It's an object lesson in independent record production. If Arthur Baker looks like he should be playing drums in a heavy-metal group, then Cory makes a credible Beach

DR JECKYL AND MR HYDE

Boy (in their younger days). With a background in DJing upstate New York, there are no doubts about his ability to spot good dance music. His confidence in Dr Jeckyl and Mr Hyde was justified by their third release ('the first two records, which we thought were great, were total stiffs') which was made in 11 days from conception to the stores. Produced extremely cheaply, it went on to sell 150,000 12-inch copies. Although the Jeckyll and Hyde duo may have been overstating their case in 'Genius Rap' when they bragged about penthouses overlooking Central Park and pictures on the cover of *Jet* and *TV Guide*, it was a success of sufficient dimensions to establish them in the easy-come, easy-go rap hall of fame.

Versions are obviously a convenient way of making records as most of the ideas have already been worked out in the original. Some of the most interesting covers are those that offer an alternative viewpoint (answer record style) to the lyrics of the existing song. Sylvia Robinson made a brief return to recording with 'Good To Be the Queen', her answer to Mel Brooks's rap 'Good To Be the King', and in Brooklyn, Reelin and Rockin' Records produced a

IF WOOD COULD RAP: WAYNE AND CHARLIE

group called Bon Rock who seemed to specialise in turning some of the conventional messages of dance music on their head.

Situated on Fort Hamilton Parkway, Reelin and Rockin' is run by Ed Pavia and Anthony Giammanco, a team who have worked together in the music business for 20 years running a Brooklyn record shop called Now Music. Pavia also gave guitar lessons and through giving concerts of his pupils realised that he and his partner might as well be making records instead of just selling them. Their first release was 'Searchin' Rap' by Bon Rock and the Rythem Rebellion. Bon Rock had appeared in the record shop from time to time and had eventually managed to convince the partners that he had talent and, in the words of Giammanco, 'the knowledge and feel of the street'.

Bon Rock's trio comprises one male and two females – Bon Rock, Tania Battiste and Diane Hawkins. 'Searchin' Rap' was a twist on the theme of Unlimited Touch's 'Searching To Find the One' on Prelude. Where Unlimited Touch, in a beautiful but lyrically dubious song, were out looking for a strong man, Tania and Diane were looking out for themselves, 'born between two 45s' and learning to cut up with the best at the Audubon Ballroom. Their 'Junior Wants to Play' (released through Tommy Boy) revamped Junior Giscombe's 'Mama Used to Say', but this time Junior was dragged away from sensible maternal advice and turned into a hip young hedonist whose attempts at sweet-talking women got him a solid 'Oh no, not tonight darlin'' rejection.

Rap was also busy plundering its own stockroom. The confusing interchangeability of MC clichés like 'shock the house' and the similar feel of much of the music made it hard enough for the casual listener to distinguish individual records, let alone choose good from bad. As with any genre, the verbal and musical crosstalk could be seen from a number of viewpoints – either it had an 'archaeological' richness which was fun to unravel or it was lost in repetition. Probably both interpretations are true. A record like Wayne and Charlie's 'Check It Out' (Sugarhill, 1981) has all the clichés, but it's interesting for being a ventriloquist and his wooden dummy offering a new (uncredited, naturally) angle on Kurtis Blow's street-smart protest 'The Breaks'. If wood could rap . . .

Other records attempted to move beyond the simple funk basis of rap and create a music that evoked turntable cutting. One of the wittiest was the Disco Four's 'Country Rock Rap'. Better known for their later electro-rap releases on Profile, the group included Bobby Robinson's son, so fittingly the record came out on Enjoy. 'Country Rock Rap' is another Pumpkin music track – a jaunty banjo hoedown with a hilarious story of yahoo-yelling cowhands leaving the farm to rock the disco till the break of dawn. King Tim III had evoked squaredance with his 'grab your partner, swing her round' lines in the very first rap record, but nobody had gone quite as hee-haw mad as The Disco Four. Naturally, it took a white person to take the idea to the top of the charts. Malcolm McLaren's 'Buffalo Gals' was undeniably more commercial than 'Country Rock Rap' but it is still depressing that the experimentation in hip hop needed opportunists, white or black, to take it into the mainstream pop charts.

The Disco Four's redneck rap, along with similar fusions like The Cold Crush Brothers' 'Punk Rock Rap', had its origins in Bronx sound systems. The breadth of music being used to create break-beat music – the fertilising ground for such records – is partially shown by Paul Winley's *Super Disco Brakes* anthologies, produced by DJ Jolly Rogers for Jolly Rogers Records (a message in there somewhere, maybe?).

Winley knew from his background in the very early discos that popular dancefloor records could be hard to find for the average punter, especially if DJs were blacking out the centre labels or soaking them off. He was also familiar with navigating 'obstacles' like copyright or union restrictions:

> I promoted a lot of shows – me and disc jockeys like Jocko. We ran shows at the Audubon. We were running discos before discos were ever popular. I'm talking about 1962. We used to call them record hops and they were eliminated to skating rinks and different places, but in a class A union ballroom you couldn't put records. I used to own a dancehall and the union wouldn't allow you to play records. Me and Jocko, we used a place called the Audubon Ballroom, 166 and Broadway, that's where Malcolm X got killed. In fact I was giving shows when Malcolm got killed that Sunday.
>
> We had trouble with the union so I had a group of fellers and we used to just grab the delegate and give him $50 and say, 'Do you wanna take this or do you wanna hang out the window?' He got to know us so he'd come up every Sunday for his 50. This went on for years and eventually disco became a very big thing.

Super Disco Brakes, a four-volume set of poorly transferred disco classics mixed with Winley product, contains tracks like 'Funky Nassau' by West Indian group The Beginning of the End (mysteriously attributed to Dyke and the Blazers on the centre label), 'Funky Drummer' by James Brown and other b boy source material by The Meters, whose New Orleans fatback funk was one of the main roots of hip-hop beats, Creative Source (disguised as Creative Service), the JBs and The Blackbyrds.

Some of the major breaks records are included – Magic Disco Machine's 'Scratchin'', Dennis Coffey's 'Scorpio', Captain Sky's 'Super Sperm' and Bob James's 'Mardi Gras'. There are two African tracks, 'Soul Makossa' (Winley was the first to jump on the New York disco craze for Manu Dibango's Cameroon Afro Quelque Chose) and 'Easy Dancin'' by Wagadu-Gu (reputed to be by Nigerian highlife star Prince Nico). Grouped together on Volume Three are Gil Scott-Heron's disco hit 'In The Bottle', a track from Lightnin' Rod's *Hustler's Convention* album on Douglas (basically a Last Poets record but credited to Alan Douglas on *Disco Brakes*) and the legendary 'Apache'.

Many of these tracks inspired later rap recordings. Bob James's cover of Paul Simon's 'Take Me to the Mardi Gras' begins with a tremendously atmospheric percussion break before lapsing into MOR sweetness. The break was the part that the b boys played, and in 1982 The Crash Crew released a single on Sugarhill called 'Breaking Bells (Take Me To the Mardi Gras)' which, despite giving writing credits to Paul Simon, bore almost no resemblance to either his song or Bob James's cover.

Captain Sky (christened Daryl L. Cameron) recorded the kind of George Clinton-inspired comic-strip funk the b boys and b girls liked. 'Super Sperm' (actually called 'Super Sporm' on the sleeve of *The Adventures of Captain Sky*, presumably for the sake of propriety) gets a namecheck in 'Rapper's Delight' and is claimed as one of the influences on Afrika Bambaataa's 'Planet Rock' along with Kraftwerk and a track called 'The Mexican'. More of 'The Mexican' later, except to say that Funky Four tried to make a decent record from it, called 'Feel It', and failed.

The record on which everybody concurs – the quintessential hip-hop track – is 'Apache' by The Incredible Bongo Band. The song was written by an English ex-grammar school boy, a singer named Jerry Lordan, and was recorded in 1960 by both guitarist Bert Weedon (strictly no relation to Dennis who played on 'Heartbeat') and instrumental group The Shadows. The Shadows' version, starring Cliff Richard on bongos, was a million seller later covered by The Ventures, an American guitar group who specialised in covering records as they started to move up the lower reaches of the charts. If a song got to the top then The Ventures could release their instrumental immediately and cash in. In 1974 The Incredible Bongo Band, a Jamaican group who had international disco hits like 'Let There Be Drums' and 'Bongo Rock '73', recorded their version. It emphasised the 'big beat' feel of the original – a bit less Hollywood Red Indian hub-a-hiya – and extended the percussion breaks into mini bongo symphonies. Cover-cover-cover versions of 'Apache', evidently oblivious to the song's past in white instrumental music, began to appear on Sugarhill in the '80s – first the Sugarhill Gang's 'Apache' and then West Street Mob (Joey Robinson Jr's group) with 'Break Dancin' – Electric Boogie'.

An underground movement indirectly inspired by a Cliff Richard percussion break might give the impression of a lemming-like abandonment of black traditions, but in a perverse way these cut-ups of unlikely records, whether by The Monkees or Yellow Magic Orchestra, were a recreation of the forthright emotion that at times looked like becoming a rarity in the mainstream of black music. They were a way of tearing the associations and the pre-packaging from finished musical product and reconstructing it, ignoring its carefully considered intentions and restitching it into new music. As the process of recording music became increasingly fragmented in the '70s – a drum track laid down in Muscle Shoals, a back-up vocal in California, a lead voice in New York – so the implication began to exist that consumers might eventually be able to rejig a track according to their own preferences.

The b boy DJs and MCs were half-way between consumers and performers (until they became stars) and their response to packaged music was to violate it with cutting and rapping. If there was a model for the final results then it was the proto-raps being played as break beats.

One of Afrika Bambaataa's favourite records is 'Tramp' by Otis Redding and Carla Thomas. It's a tune with an intense Southern feel – the lyrics (written by bluesmen Lowell Fulsom and Jimmy McCracklin) have a familiar theme. Carla pours scorn on Otis for his rural Southern ways, his overalls, his boots and his long hair. Otis roars back his defence over Al

Jackson's funky drum breaks, offering Carla a choice of rat, squirrel or frog in return for her demands of mink and sable. Basically a talking record, it is a satire that harks back to the husband and wife comedy teams – Butterbeans and Susie or Stringbeans and Sweetie May – or the venomous dialogue of songs such as Big Maybelle's 'Gabbin' Blues' from 1952. The imposing Maybelle is being tormented by a gossip – 'here comes ol' evil chick, always telling everybody she come from Chicago. Got Mississippi written all over her'. Her defence, like Otis's, was her pride and the threatening power of her awesome voice.

No matter how far Bambaataa and others like him may go in their outlandish selections of source material or their desire for internationalism, the music always returns to two basic elements – a funky drumbeat and some spoken or chanted words. Both spring from an abundant Afro-American tradition.

9. Tough

The release of two Last Poets records in March of 1984 was a reminder, should one be necessary, that rap had very recent predecessors. Both releases were 12-inch singles – 'Super Horror Show' by the Last Poet and 'Long Enough' by The Last Poets. A different last poet was behind each record – 'Long Enough' by Jalaluddin Mansur Nuriddin on a Brooklyn label called Kee Wee, and 'Super Horror Show' by Abiodun Oyewole on Nia, a label normally associated with Captain Rock and the Fantastic Aleems production team. With a percussion intro reminiscent of early Last Poets records, a strong synthesiser/beat-box music track and an 'I've had it' lyric, 'Long Enough' is the stronger of the two. Ironically, 'Super Horror Show' is a pale imitation of 'The Message', the Grandmaster Flash and the Furious Five hit of 1982 which set the ball rolling for the message rap fad through its enormous international success.

By the time The Last Poets were interviewed by Jonathon Cott for *Rolling Stone* magazine in 1970, Abiodun Oyewole had left the group. He can be heard on their first album for Douglas, a New York company run by Alan Douglas who also recorded music by John McLaughlin and Jimi Hendrix. The Harlem-based Poets were at

THRILLER BREAKER AT THE ROXY

that time Alafia Pudim, Omar Ben Hassan and Nilaja, the percussionist (all of them later changed their names). They described themselves as being part of a new age for poets – prophetic of the way in which wall poems and street verse would be set to dance-music tracks and climb not only the R&B charts but also pop hit parades all over the world.

There was little chance of the same success coming to The Last Poets when they released titles like 'Niggers Are Scared of Revolution' or 'White Man's Got a God Complex'. They took streetcorner rap with its potential for verbal violence and used it as an assault on what they saw as black apathy, self-exploitation and stereotyped roles. Direct or indirect, it was an attack on white society also, and Nilaja is quoted as saying, 'If I were white I wouldn't come hear us. Just like I wouldn't go hear George Wallace.'

Their ancestry lay in the tough-voiced black writers who had earlier set poetry in a musical context or used lyrics and music to create a specifically political message – Imamu Amiri Baraka's 'Black Dada Nihilismus' with The New York Art Quartet, recorded in 1965, as well as his work with Sun Ra; Archie Shepp's poems for Malcolm X, 'Malcolm, Malcolm, Semper Malcolm' from his Impulse album *Fire Music* and 'Poem For Malcolm' recorded in Paris in the late '60s; the Abbey Lincoln/Max Roach collaborations including *We Insist – The Freedom Now Suite* recorded for Candid, and, going back to before the '60s Civil Rights battles, a moving set of recordings of Langston Hughes reading his poetry with two jazz groups – one including Red Allen and Vic Dickenson, the other with Charles Mingus and Shafi Hadi.

The Last Poets were virtually the sole occupants of a lonely territory between the jazz poets and the commercial singers who had spoken out during the decade of Civil Rights and Black Nationalism – Nina Simone, James Brown, Curtis Mayfield. Their poems reflected their position – 'Uncle Sam's Lament' from the *At Last* album mixes free jazz with references to James Brown's 'Ain't It Funky' and Jimmy Castor's 'Hey Leroy, Your Mama's Callin'', and one of their hardest tracks, 'This Is Madness', is full of references to 'Trane, Bird and King Pleasure's 'I'm In the Mood for Love'.

In *Die Nigger Die*, H Rap Brown, ex-minister of justice in the Black Panthers and chairman of the SNCC (Student National Co-ordinating Committee), wrote: 'The street is where young bloods get their education. I learned how to talk in the street, not from reading about Dick and Jane going to the zoo and all that simple shit. The teacher would test our vocabulary each week, but we knew the vocabulary we needed. They'd give us arithmetic to exercise our minds. Hell, we exercised our minds by playing the dozens'.

Jonathon Cott's *Rolling Stone* feature, 'The Last Poets and Apocalypse', makes a similar point:

> But what The Last Poets do onstage is nothing more than heighten the form of a new Black urban street poetry. At a New

> York high school assembly commemorating Malcolm X's death two months ago, the 'predominantly Black' students hooted the principal down, and kids got up on stage and read their poems – charged statements like those of The Poets, rhythmically asserting black consciousness while revealing the breakdown and proving unworkable the New York City school system.

The Last Poets made their streetlife connection clear with an album called *Hustlers Convention* (attributed to Lightnin' Rod) released on Douglas in 1973.

Hustlers Convention is a modern-day toast, the story of a gambler, Sport, and his crime partner, Spoon, who win at craps, pool and poker at a hustlers' convention in Hamhock's Hall. The story ends with Sport freed from a 12-year stretch on Sing Sing's death row after a shoot-out with the cops. By the time he's released he has had time to think about the foolishness of being a small-time hustler.

Music on the album is provided by an impressive list of names including Kool and the Gang and Eric Gale; with its sound effects and atmosphere it brings to mind other black audio-dramas like *Roi Boye and the Gotham Minstrels* by saxophonist Julius Hemphill (one of the musicians on *Hustlers Convention*), David Porter's *Victim of the Joke* soul opera and Melvin Van Peebles's soundtrack albums *Sweet Sweetback's Baadasssss Song* and *Don't Play Us Cheap*.

In the middle '70s, *Hustlers Convention* was being used as a break record by hip-hop DJs. They were also using Gil Scott-Heron tracks. Both Gil Scott-Heron and The Last Poets are seen by most Bronx rappers as the godfathers of the message rap. As a writer, Scott-Heron published novels and a rap poem – 'Small Talk at 125th and Lennox' – before putting the words into a musical context. Early rap poems such as 'Sex Education: Ghetto Style' and 'Whitey On the Moon' were in The Last Poets mould (though strong in their own right) with conga backup. Other raps like 'The Revolution Will Not Be Televised' used more instruments (drums, bass, flute) but they were still hard-hitting political broadsides which contrasted sharply with his mellow and melancholic songs. The content was the same in both, but the effectiveness of the rap format was driven home by the release of the *Reflections* album in 1982, with its rap attack on Ronald Reagan in 'B Movie'.

At Tuff City Records in the strictly B movie landscape of Long Island City, Aaron Fuchs – long-time R&B collector and writer of the Motown chapters in Allan Betrock's *Girl Groups* book – is being forthright about an aspect of rap he disdains:

AARON FUCHS: TUFF CITY HEADQUARTERS

The only trend I do not like in rap right now is the message rap. I consider the message rap the equivalent of what strings were to rock 'n' roll in the late '50s – a capitulation to the adult norm who can't accept the music on its own terms. The people who considered 'Sixty Minute Man' by Billy Ward and the Dominoes, 'Annie Had a Baby' – as the pinnacles of '50s R&B now are super uptight over the – in quotes – hotel/motel lyrics of rap. Rap is definitely as true to the essence of rock 'n roll as anything that's out there today.

Although Kurtis Blow recorded a couple of message raps in 1980 ('The Breaks' and 'Hard Times'), it was Grandmaster Flash and the Furious Five at Sugarhill who turned it into a trend. 'The Message' appeared in the late summer of 1982. It was partly a response to Afrika Bambaataa's 'Planet Rock', a record that came from behind the frontrunners and left them all standing. Instead of moving with the Kraftwerk-influenced sound, 'The Message' used a backing track more in line with groups like D Train and The Jammers – a hard, slowish beat that was electronic enough to drag Sugarhill into the new age of dance music. Mostly the creation of Ed Fletcher (known as Duke Bootee) and Melvin Glover (Melle Mel), it recycled a number of lines from 'Superrappin'' but was otherwise a strikingly original song which combined shock images of violent and decaying New York with enough melodic and percussive hooks to make it a highly commercial proposition.

It has always been debatable just how much listeners take in the lyrics of songs. Sung vocals have a tendency to blend into the instrumental music, so that often the only words that are remembered are those in the title. For obvious reasons this problem is even bigger in dance music. Rap vocals, on the other hand, have a separation from the music – it is possible to communicate in more detail and with a greater directness. 'The Message' managed to harness this potential to a pop sensibility as well as a hardcore dance track. It cut straight across the stagnation in rap lyricism.

Rap before 'The Message' wasn't all hotel/motel/Mercedes/young ladies. Aside from Kurtis Blow, there were records here and there which went beyond bragging and boasting. Community People's 'Education Wrap' on Delmar Donnell's Delmar International Records updated James Brown's 'kids, stay in school' lecture, and Sweet Tee's 'Vicious Rap' showed that there was one kid who was 'gonna scream and shout and let the government know what we all about'. The toughest talk, though, came from Brother D with his 'How We Gonna Make the Black Nation Rise', a release on Clappers. The Clappers label was started by Lister Hewan Lowe, a Jamaican who had moved to New York after working with Augustus Pablo on the Yard Music label. Brother D, a young maths teacher named Daryl Aamaa Nubyahn, recorded a hip-hop tune to reflect the philosophy of a political and cultural organisation called National Black Science, realising that despite rap's being the happening music in his neighbourhood of the Bronx, it wasn't saying

MELLE MEL AT THE ROXY

much beyond personality commercials. Taking one of the two most popular rhythms of the time, Cheryl Lynn's 'Got To Be Real', Brother D produced something that was a considerable departure from the usual formula:

The Ku Klux Klan is on the loose,
Training their kids in machine gun use.
The story might give you stomach cramps
Like America's got concentration camps.
While you're partyin' on on on on and on,
The others may be hot by the break of dawn.
The party may end one day soon,
When they're rounding niggers up in the afternoon.

Another Clappers release was 'Ms D.J. Rap It Up!' by She. She has a lot of faces. On the subway she is liable to be recognised because of her role as Thomasina in NBC's daytime TV soap opera *Another World*, but she also goes under the name Ms D.J. as well as her legal name, Sheila Spencer. A church choir singer in Brooklyn from the age of five until her late teens, Sheila is a trained actress who has also provided background paaardddy vocals for Kurtis Blow's first album and worked as a Muhammad Ali boxing cheerleader (an admirable training for an MC). Her record was a conscious attempt by her producer, Dennis Weeden, to get a solo female rapper onto the market.

Though rapping is a macho stronghold there have been a few women with lyrics that struck back. Sula's 'Jungle Rap' asked Tarzan why he had to play with such a hard

MS DJ RAP IT UP: SHEILA SPENCER

hand, and Lady B told her story of how she and Superman had a fight and she hit him in the head with some kryptonite. Lady B's record was first released on a Philadelphia label called Tec, mixed by Nick Martinelli (now well known for his mixing collaborations with David Todd on West End) and then picked up by Sugarhill and re-released in a slightly speeded-up version. Called 'To The Beat Y'all' it also told a tale of Jack and Jill going up the hill to play but ending up with a baby because 'stupid' Jill forgot the pill. Sequence came straight back with their 'Simon Says' – a warning about boys who want to 'pump' every day but refuse to take responsibility for the babies they help to create. It also took a few lines from 'The Clapping Song', the Shirley Ellis song that went gold in the mid '60s.

Shirley Ellis, along with her writer Lincoln Chase, was another forerunner of rap. The wordplay songs, 'The Name Game' and 'Ever See a Diver Kiss His Wife While the Bubbles Bounce About Above the Water', were nearly 20 years ahead of Z-language raps like Frankie Smith's 'Double Dutch Bus', UTFO's 'Beats and Rhymes' or graffiti artist Rammelzee's tricknology rap 'Beat Bop'. The Kangol Kid, one half of UTFO, is a breaker and popper who specialises in what he calls 'disability moves'. UTFO dance with Brooklyn rap group Whodini but they also rap themselves. Kangol explains the word game behind their first record: 'Another new thing is Z-rap. It'd be like a code language. I would talk to him and his name's Doctor Ice. I would say, "Dizoctor Izice. Yizo hizo bizoy wizon't youza kizoy mesover herezere?" – that's just saying, "Yo, home boy, why don't you come over here?" and what I did is make a rap out of that language. In New York they'd understand but Europe they just have to get up on it now'.

'Beat Bop' by Rammelzee Vs. K-Rob was initially released as a limited pressing by artist Jean Michel Basquiat on Tartown and then picked up by Profile Records for wider distribution. Rammelzee's name is a conjunction of Ramm-elevation-Z (Z being a symbol of energy which flows in two directions); his graffiti paintings and drawings are unusual even for the hip-hop art scene. 'Beat Bop' is rapped in what he calls slanguage – a stream of consciousness rap between a gangster and a child who debate the pros and cons of school. The music is a slow trance beat drenched in washes of echo which drop and clear like mist – the nearest parallel is the hypnotic Yoruban Fuji, Apala and Waka drumbeat musics from Nigeria. The language glides bafflingly in

FLASH, RAHEIM, KID CREOLE AND THE NEW RECRUITS

and out of hip-hop cliché, social realism and pure nonsense – Rammelzee, the Screamin' Jay Hawkins of rap:

> *Bunny rock a ya don't stop,*
> *That long fingernail at the end of my tail*
> *Oh my pinky cocaine make it slip-a-my lip,*
> *Just make you freak when the paniwani was flip*
> *Like the little pat to the dab'll make you my hip.*
> *Shake shake rock body rock a hip an-a-hop,*
> *Like a – RTMs my –*
> *Nose don't care about the rhythm that breaks.*
> (approximate transcription)

Profile also released 'Street Justice' by The Rake (known to his family as Keith Rose). It was a story rap which ignored the clichés and the nonsense and went for the social realism. Amazingly enough, this grim scenario of a vigilante bent on revenge after his wife is raped and the attackers are let off was written by two professional songwriters, Blatt and Gottleib, who wrote 'She Was My Girl' for The Four Tops. 'Street Justice' was fairly typical of the subject matter current in rap after 'The Message'. The follow-up to 'The Message' was another Ed Fletcher/Melle Mel collaboration called 'Message 2 (Survival)'. With hindsight it was the first sign of the imminent split within Grandmaster Flash and the Furious Five, though Sylvia Robinson's insistence on

Melvin's rapping solo on 'The Message' was the beginning of divide and rule. 'Message 2' was in the style of the sequels and prequels that had become an obsession in cinema. More *Halloween II* than *Rocky III*, it was bad news in more ways than one. Chic's 'Good Times' had finally been replaced (commercially) by the hard times.

It has been suggested that record companies go through phases of releasing songs with political or protest lyrics and that 1982 onward is one such phase. Distinguishing worthwhile bandwagon jumping from sheer cynical opportunism can be tricky – besides which, the eventual effect of a record can be very different from the original intentions, good or bad. Among the more incisive high-pressure raps which were thrown up by message-ism were 'The Bottom Line' by South Bronx on Rissa Chrissa, 'Problems of the World' by The Fearless Four (very striking lyrics by DLB), 'You Gotta Believe' by 'Love Bug' Starski (more survivalism than protest) on The Fever label, 'Bad Times (I Can't Stand It)' by Captain Rapp on Becket Records, 'It's Life (You Gotta Think Twice)' by Rock Master Scott and the Dynamic 3, and Run-D.M.C.'s 'Hard Times', both on Profile.

The contradictions of a money-minded craze for gory social realism and criticism of the Reagan administration, with its callous cutbacks in social programmes, are hard to resolve. The juxtaposition of protests about rape victims with rampant machismo or hard-times lyrics sung by kids in expensive leather outfits and gold chains can be hard to stomach. With Jesse Jackson's decision to campaign for the 1984 Democratic nomination in the race for presidency came a new mood in American black politics. The long-overdue granting of a commemoration day for Martin Luther King led to the release of Stevie Wonder's tribute, 'Happy Birthday', with a B side of the Civil Rights campaigner's speeches, including 'I Have a Dream'. Also from the soulside came a tribute from Bobby Womack, and in the rap field, reflecting the hip-hop technique of overlaying beats with speeches by black leaders, came 'Martin Luther', a Kraftwerk-meets-desert-funk-and-black-politics 12 inch by the Las Vegas-based Hurt 'Em Bad and the S.C. Band.

The Jesse Jackson campaign was supported by Face 2000 with 'Run Jesse Run' and Melle Mel with 'Jesse', the latter a collaboration between Melvin Glover, Reggie Griffin, Sylvia Robinson and one of The Isley Brothers, reflecting the Isleys' business tie-ups with Sugarhill. Most surprising of all was the late 1983 posthumous release by Malcolm X on Tommy Boy Records. The record was a hard beat-box track put together by ex-staff drummer at Sugarhill, Keith LeBlanc, with equally ferocious speeches by Malcolm X. Inevitably, it trailed controversy in its wake, with a court battle between Sugarhill and Tommy Boy over legal rights to the speeches and dissenting voices from within the black community about the disrespect they felt the record showed to one of their leaders. Paul Winley, who had released speeches by both Martin Luther King and Malcolm X, had this to say: 'It's just like taking one of your idols, one of your heroes and boogie-ing behind 'em. It's just like taking the Pope's speech and putting some disco music behind it – here's John Paul, baby!' Others felt that Black Nationalism from a white drummer and a white record company was an insult.

Nevertheless, it was sanctioned by Dr Betty Shabazz, the widow of Malcolm X, and caught the mood of its time perfectly. 'No Sell Out', along with Afrika Bambaataa's rebel optimism of 'Renegades of Funk' and the militant break music from the hip-hop minimalists, were the strongest contenders in the new spirit of 1984 punk.

10. Whiplash snuffs the candle flame

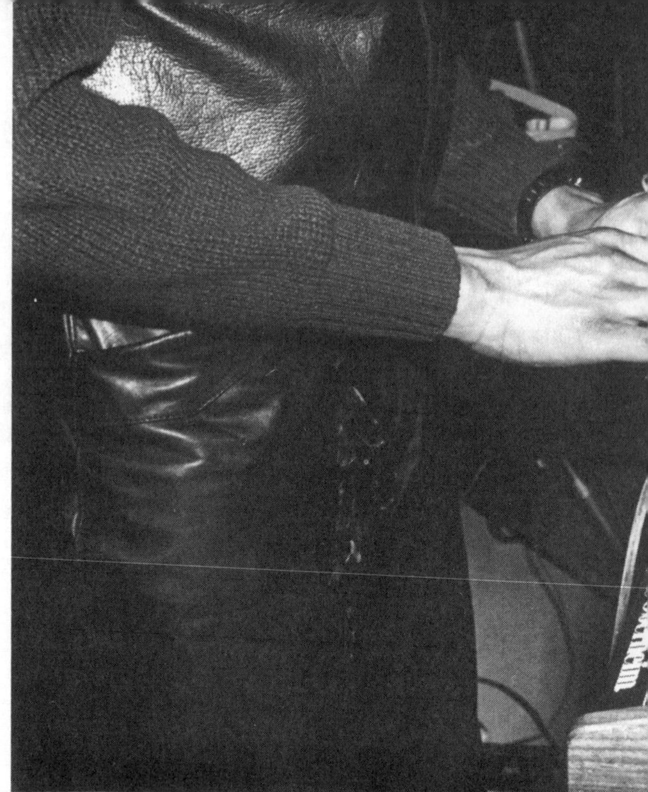

ROCKIN' TO THE SOUNDS OF THE BEATBOX

Fresh as the first rap records were, they were tame compared to the uncensored beats and rhymes of the parks and high schools. What was a DJ to do on a record? 'Superrappin'' threw a clue into the wind but nobody caught it – The Furious Five chant 'Flash is on the beat box' but the drum machine stays mute. Funk was still powered by a set of traps. Flash was a pioneer in combining turntable trickery with beat-box improvisations, using an ancient keyboard percussion box made by Vox, an English company whose name can be spotted on the amplifiers in old footage of The Beatles. It was a bootleg record that pulled electronic drums out of the Bronx. 'Flash To the Beat' by Flash and the Five on Bozo Meko Records was recorded off the sound system at Bronx River Community Centre by Afrika Bambaataa. It puts most so-called noise records to shame.

The response at Sugarhill was to rush the group into the studio to record an official version. 'Flash To the Beat' (Sugarhill) is less celebrated than Flash and the Furious Five hits but is nonetheless superb. For nearly six minutes the Furious Five trade off catch phrases, parodies of Brit-speak (a great source of amusement to rappers), solo singing and unison chants against a seething beats-only backdrop of drums, Latin percussion and Flash's chattering, popping percussion box fed through an echo delay. At five minutes 50 seconds the group start to sing 'the bass is with the beat box playing' and in crashes Doug Wimbish with a vicious riff that stays with the record for the remaining five minutes.

Despite many claims to the contrary, much of the early serious use of drum machines was in black music. Electronic rhythms were mostly an accessory for organists (the kind of thing heard on Timmy Thomas's 'Why Can't We Live Together') but in the early '70s two musicians in particular, Sly Stone and Stevie Wonder, used drum machines as a part of finding greater independence – learning to exploit new technology and the developing multi-track

studio facilities to further it. Sylvia Robinson and The Moments were also up there among the earliest musicians to record with drum machines so it's hard to know why it took them so long to get around to recording 'Flash To the Beat'.

Sly Stone used the drum box extensively to build up tracks, playing most of the instruments, including acoustic drums, himself, and then deciding whether to leave the machine in or out of the final mixdown. *There's A Riot Going On* (Epic, 1971), Sly's druggy masterpiece, is characterised by the drum-machine sound. On songs like 'Time', 'Spaced Cowboy', 'Family Affair' and 'Africa Talks To You "The Asphalt Jungle"' it ticks, hisses and tocks away at an almost insulting volume, sometimes almost drowning out the mumbled vocals. It imbues the songs with a mechanical feeling which only adds to the sense of alienation throughout the whole album. The drum box mixes perfectly with Larry Graham's slapping and popping bass (also way ahead of its time), but the personal mix in the group was less than happy and Graham left shortly after contributing uncredited work to the follow-up album, *Fresh*, and formed his own group.

Graham Central Station pursued many of the ideals of The Family Stone – musicians of mixed race and gender playing rock-tinged heavyweight funk – and on a track called 'The Jam' from 1975 one of the lead vocalists, Patryce 'Chocolate' Banks, takes what may have been the first drum-machine solo in record history:

Uh F. U. N. K. box
It's an F. U. N. K. box-box-ah
Play it on a funk box y'all
My name is C. H. O. C. L. E. T.
Chocolate.

'The Jam' was a favourite b boy break record, as were many Sly and the Family Stone cuts. Sly's coke- and smack-brained ideas made a big impression in the asphalt jungles of New York (although musically speaking only – hard drugs were mostly disapproved of). On top of that the drum machine was the perfect instrument to blend into the concept of an MC show. Plug it in by the record decks and the DJ could move from one set of controls to the other without losing the flow. Flash was honing

GRANDMASTERS – MARQUEE IN TIMES SQUARE

the combined arts of cutting, scratching and manually operated beat box. Being a DJ was starting to look like an Olympics event. Flash tells the story of his name:

> Somebody was telling me that there a Grandmaster Flowers out there before me but I was named that from my fans. It was '74, on my birthday. There was this guy named Joe Kid. He was one of the troublemakers in my party but he was a good friend of mine. He said, 'Flash, for the way that you play you can't just call yourself DJ Flash. Grandmaster sounds great, man. You should put it on top of that.' After I took the title I knew I had to start going to a laboratory, so to speak, and invent new ideas.

KRAFTWERK: DO THE FUNKY ROBOT

Grandmaster was an appropriate name for the extremes of concentration, dexterity and physical precision required to stay on top of the competition. As Flash had said elsewhere, if you made too many mistakes you could get yourself shot!

In the barren setting of a school gymnasium the fantasy level of the music invoked a mythical battle between the DC Comics superhero Flash, the fastest man alive, and the Shaolin grandmasters with their Mantis Fists, Drunken swordplay and Hawk's Paw Kung Fu. A crazy cast of one-armed boxers, deaf and mute heroines and white-eyebrow monks merged with the strangely costumed alter ego of police scientist Barry Allen, The Flash. When the smoke cleared a new superhero emerged – Grandmaster Flash – and a host of imitators followed in his wake – The Ghost of Flash, Grandmaster Caz, Grand Wizard Theodore and, the final ignominy, a fake Grandmaster Flash appearing with Melle Mel after the split of the group in late 1983.

Hong Kong martial arts films took over from the craze for blaxploitation movies in the early '70s. Even now, Grandmaster films are still shown in the cinemas lining Times Square, alongside Japanese ninja pictures, the latest Clint Eastwood Dirty Harry instalment and a mixed bunch of porno productions. In his book *Black Film as Genre*, Thomas Cripps assesses the appeal of Chinese films to black youth in America:

> The young black audiences who had originally supported 'blaxploitation' films soon lost interest and shifted their allegiance to other genres including science fiction or martial arts films, which traded on violent revenge themes set in Oriental locales. Black youth, then, recoiled from fantasies of lust and power, choosing instead symbols from another culture that provided metaphors for Afro-American experience despite their Oriental settings. Martial arts films offered blacks comic strips of pure vengeance dramatized in a choreography of violence unobtainable within the literal context of American social realism.

Sharing the twilight zone of 42nd Street movie houses, drug dealers and seedy subterranean record stores are the video arcades. Video games have had a big influence on latter day hip hop – the arcades are bleeping, pulsing, 24-hour refuges for the obsessive vidkids with nowhere else to go. Since the Japanese exploitation of American Nolan Bushnell's original games, a major part of the populated world has been saturated with Space Invaders, Gorgars, Missile Commands, Dragon's Lairs and Ms Pacmans. Along with their addictive properties, their imagery and their insatiable appetite for coins goes an e-z-learn induction into the world of computer technology.

CHOREOGRAPHY OF VIOLENCE

On side two of the notorious 'Death Mix', recorded live at James Monroe High School in the Bronx, Afrika Bambaataa and Jazzy Jay can be heard cutting up YMO's (Yellow Magic Orchestra's) 'Firecracker'. 'Firecracker' is an electronic cover version of a Martin Denny tune (Denny, a white American based in Hawaii, specialises in exotic easy-listening music), and on the 1979 album from which it is taken it segues out of a track called 'Computer Games', a maddening simulation of video-

PLAYLAND ARCADE, TIMES SQUARE

machine beeps, rumbles and banal tunes.

Along with YMO, Bambaataa had a taste for Gary Numan ('Cars' is enjoyed by other hip hoppers, for some unknown reason) and Kraftwerk. Kraftwerk managed to invade almost all record-buying markets in America, from easy-listening to R&B. Bam recalls their influence:

> Kraftwerk – I don't think they even knew how big they were among the black masses back in '77 when they came out with 'Trans-Europe Express'. When that came out I thought that was one of the best and weirdest records I ever heard in my life. I said, 'scuse the expression, this is some weird shit! Everybody just went crazy off of that. I guess they found out when they came over and did a performance at the Ritz how big they was. They had four encores and people would not let them leave. That's an amazing group to see – just to see what computers and all that can do. They took like calculators and added something to it – people pressing it and start playing it like music. It was funky. I started looking at telephones – the push-button type – they really mastered those industrial type of machines.

Kraftwerk were the most unlikely group to create such an effect among young blacks. Four be-suited showroom dummies who barely moved a muscle when they played, they were nonetheless the first group using pure electronics to achieve anything like the rhythmic sophistication of quality black dance music. They were fascinating to kids who had grown up with the incursion of microchip technology into everyday life. The George Clinton funk empire and its theatre of excesses had taken sex, sci-fi and comic-book abandonment about as far it could go on stage; four Aryan robots pressing buttons was a joke at the other extreme.

The album version of 'Trans-Europe Express' is extremely long – 13 minutes 32 seconds in total. With its eerie dramatic atmosphere, constant changes of texture and vocoder-type vocals on absolutely regular medium-tempo beats, it was unwittingly a b boy classic. Bambaataa was overlaying speeches by Malcolm X and other Nation of Islam ministers or Martin Luther King, and for Flash it was one of the very few records he was prepared to leave running for its entire length without cutting or scratching: ' "Trans-Europe Express", that was one record you couldn't too much cut – it was cutting itself. That shit was jumping off – leave that shit alone – smoke a cigarette. You can go cool out – go to the bathroom.'

For a Tommy Boy Records follow-up to 'Jazzy Sensation', Afrika Bambaataa took musical elements from 'Trans-Europe Express' – specifically the rhythmic feel and the simple melody line – as well as rhythm ideas from Kraftwerk's 'Numbers' and Captain Sky's 'Super Sperm'. Another inspiration was a record called 'The Mexican', a rock guitar treatment of Ennio Morricone's theme for Sergio Leone's film of greed and retribution, *For a Few Dollars More*. In his book *Spaghetti Westerns*,

Christopher Frayling describes Morricone's film scores as being 'as if Duane Eddy had bumped into Rodrigo, in the middle of a crowded Via Veneto' – very hip hop.

'The Mexican' was released on a West End Records Euro-disco album called *Bombers*. A 12-minute track with extremely long percussion breaks, it was 'interpolated' by guitarist Alan Shacklock, the main mover behind an English progressive rock band called Babe Ruth. Babe Ruth recorded their own limp dancebeat version of 'For a Few Dollars More' in 1972 and Bambaataa had been cutting between these two records and Kraftwerk on the turntables. The feature they shared in common was the tension of a melodramatic, drawn-out melody laid over a beat – also the most unusual aspect of 'Planet Rock', the name of the record which emerged from this Frankenstein process.

'Planet Rock' was so strange on first hearing that it was hard to believe anybody would buy it. Not only one of the massive hits of 1982, it also shifted dance music into another gear. Produced by a team of Bambaataa, MC group Sonic Force (Mr Biggs, G.L.O.B.E. and Pow Wow), producer Arthur Baker and keyboardist John Robie, it combined a party atmosphere with propulsive electronic percussion or loud scratch-effect accents which sounded like an orchestra being rocketed into outer space. From the opening moments of Bambaataa shouting, 'Party people, party people – can y'all get funky?', 'Planet Rock' is as addictive and as hypnotic as a two-screen miniature Donkey Kong.

It was the first record to feature Soul Sonic Force properly. G.L.O.B.E. was the

A FRANTIC SITUATION:
ARTHUR BAKER, SOUL SONIC FORCE, SHANGO AND AFRIKA BAMBAATAA AT SHAKEDOWN SOUND

inventor of the delayed-action rap called MC popping – like the Turtle Man in the Flash comic, you leave gaps in between words and phrases (not necessarily in the most obvious places). The writer of many of the Soul Sonic lyrics, G.L.O.B.E. met Bam when he was at Bronx River High School. He originally wanted to join the Funky Four but as they were already established he tried Bambaataa:

> I met up with Pow Wow. He always used to hear me rapping in the park and we would rap together. We were really friends. So then Pow Wow said, 'Okay, let's go to Bronx River' with a song that I wrote. Bam heard it and liked it and they put me on. It began with eight rappers. Then, when I came on, everybody dropped off except Mr Biggs, Pow Wow, Lisa Lee, Hutch and Ice Ice. As time went on Ice Ice fell off, then Hutch Hutch fell off then Lisa Lee fell off into The Cosmic Force. Ever since then it's been Mr Biggs, Pow Wow and G.L.O.B.E. in Soul Sonic Force.
>
> I don't even call my stuff rapping. I call it MC popping. It came along on just practising every day. For hours I was just walking around the house. I'd rap when I was washing the dishes. In the shower – like people will always sing in the shower. This was before rap records were even thought of – around '76, '77.

At the Funhouse on 26th Street, 'Looking For the Perfect Beat', Soul Sonic's follow-up to 'Planet Rock', is crashing out its idealistic message at terrific volume. The lights are flashing on and off, highlighting the fairground atmosphere of the place. The clientele are extremely young, mostly Hispanic and Italian (blacks are said to be discouraged) and the music they come to dance to is the jittering electric funk that has followed in the wake of 'Planet Rock'. Inside the DJ booth – a huge clown face – is John 'Jellybean' Benitez, yet another DJ turned producer. Jellybean's talent for creating commercial mixes out of tapes with a video-game aesthetic has been one of the factors responsible for bring hip hop downtown and, by extension, into the international marketplace. Afrika Bambaataa talks about the percolation through to lower Manhattan:

> Cassette tapes used to be our albums before anybody recorded what they called rap records. People started hearing all this rapping coming out of boxes. When they heard the tapes down in the Village they wanted to know, 'Who's this black DJ who's playing all this rock and new wave up in the Bronx?' and I was the only one who was playing all these different forms of music. They invited me downtown to play and I started in this club – The Mudd Club – then somebody called Malcolm McLaren visited us up in my home in the development projects at Bronx River. He liked what he saw so he invited my group to be on a show with Bow Wow Wow at The Ritz.
>
> That's the time the scene was really getting to know about rapping down there. They knew Grandmaster Flash already 'cos Flash had a better manage-

ment team that always looked out for him. The press jumped behind him so they always look to him like he was the first thing out there. I didn't trust nobody at the time. I was more independent than the other DJs. I didn't let nobody touch me. I guided my own career along with Soul Sonic Force and all the other groups that were under my Zulu Nation. I always worked from the streets. I made a following within the street itself – that's how I built on Zulu. I didn't have to worry about going downtown. I had my own steady crowd.

When they heard the tapes they started inviting me to play The Mudd Club, The Ritz, The Peppermint Lounge and I started getting a large white following. I ended up in Negril with Michael Holman and Lady Blue. Thursday nights there became one of the biggest nights downtown. Then it got too big for Negril. One time the fire marshalls closed the whole place down so we moved it to Danceteria. Then it got too big for Danceteria. Finally, we made home at The Roxy. It started slow building at The Roxy, and now Friday nights it's always 3,000, 4,000. Then it became a big commercial thing. Movie stars were coming, singers, everybody was coming to The Roxy and it just started stretching and stretching.

Other events which moved hip hop out of the Bronx and Harlem were shows like The Ritz rap party in March of 1981, The Funky Four's participation in a video and tour organised by The Kitchen (an art venue),

GIRLS IN THE BATHROOM AT THE FUNHOUSE

THE FUNHOUSE

and the white rap records from groups like Blondie and Tom Tom Club. Rap was irresistible as a genuine street culture created by disaffected youth. It had the double virtues of being romantic and daring yet easily packaged. Mostly it packaged itself as a self-contained show with DJs, MCs, on-the-spot graphics from graffiti artists, electric boogie and breakdancing, and maybe some double-dutch skip-rope routines.

Press coverage was unprecedented and rap tunes began to appear from all corners of the entertainment field – music, comedy and politics. The major problem with copying black music – the vocals – was largely sidestepped as almost anybody could be coached into talking their way through a rhythm.

Even the notorious entrepreneur Malcolm McLaren, previously manager for The New York Dolls, The Sex Pistols and Bow Wow Wow, took a hip hop-inspired melange of rap, Latin, Appalachian and Zulu music and with the help of WHBI radio rappers and scratchers The World's Famous Supreme Team and producer Trevor Horn, made himself a solo success. In 1983 the fad was spread even further by Charlie Ahearn's immensely likeable dramatised documentary film *Wildstyle* and the eminently dislikeable blockbuster movie *Flashdance*, and in '84 came the *Breakdance*, *Beat Street* deluge. Ten years on, hip hop had finally reached the mass international market.

The all-electronic sound of 'Planet Rock' was to become the new sound of the streets. The extraordinary advances in electronic music technology in the late '70s and early

DOUBLE DUTCH *Photo: courtesy of Stuart Cosgrove*

'80s radically transformed the possibilities for making music. Drum machines like the Roland 808, an analog machine with a microprocessor memory, along with more sophisticated (and costly) digital machines like the Linn Drum and the Oberheim DMX, compact polyphonic synthesisers and Simmons electric drums made it simple for one musician to lay down high-quality tracks without moving from the recording studio control room.

One of the records which followed quickly in the wake of 'Planet Rock' was The Fearless Four's 'Rockin' It' on Enjoy. Their previous release for Bobby Robinson was a tune called 'It's Magic', a suspended riff based on a Cat Stevens song, but it was 'Rockin' It' which really distinguished them from the crowd. From its spooky opening, 'They're here' – a catch phrase and advertising slogan from the Tobe Hooper/Steven Spielberg horror movie *Poltergeist* – it was obviously something special. A lopsided synthesiser riff stolen from Kraftwerk's 'The Man Machine' and repeated 137 times (as usual played by Pumpkin) and a battering electric drum beat were just about the only constituents other than the rap, but it was a compelling sound that captured the mood of the twitching would-be androids and vid-kids doing the electric boogie. The Fearless Four unravel their convoluted history:

Master O.C. It was about eight years ago – it started with me and Tito. We was doing home tapes, selling them for $10 in the streets. People liked Tito's voice and my cutting at that time.

Tito We had auditions to see who could be

down with our group. We were selling tapes and the tapes were giving us clientele, which means being known well.

Master O.C. We were known as The Houserockers Crew.

Tito We were selling them in Manhattan, Queens, The Bronx and our tapes was real familiar until we started really getting juice, which is people knowing us. We had got somebody else – Mike Ski – he was good. He had a different style of rap than I have. As time went by we bumped into Peso, and Peso came with a singing style of rap.

Master O.C. At that time, when Peso got down, we had Troy B from The Disco Four with us also and that's what made it four at the time. We got rid of Troy B and we found DLB when we did a talent show. We sounded good together so it was the four – me, Tito, Peso, DLB and Mike Ski at that time. At one time it was The Fearless Five.

Mike C Mike Ski had left the group. He got married and his married life couldn't cope with his career so it was The Fearless Four. We've been together ever since – pushing hits.

When rap groups call themselves the Four or the Five it doesn't always mean that there are four or five of them. The DJs tend to get left out of the numbering process – The Fearless Four feature The Mighty Mike C, The Devastating Tito, The Great Peso and DLB, The Microphone Wizard, upfront. Working the turntables behind them they have Krazy Eddie, named after the retail store with the lunatic commercials, and the Master O.C., who also produces groups like The Fantasy Three, with their 'Biters In the City'. They talk about the records they were using for beats before they recorded:

O.C. We was using jazz records. Bob James, Grover Washington, Herbie Hancock – *Headhunters* – Isaac Hayes. We was using all the old records that we could make a beat out of.

Peso Kraftwerk – that's our soul group.

Tito We were always looking in all the music – jazz and pop and all that. We were looking at records just by name like on *Headhunters. Headhunters?* Maybe it's got some beat on it. We bought *Headhunters* and found that the beat on it was something that we started loving, making songs and routines to it. We used one cut. All we did was just cut up that one part – tik tik-atik boom da boom chh doom da doom chh. We had two turntables and just kept cutting up that one beat. It sounds like a whole different record.

Following 'Rockin' It' they moved from Enjoy (as did everybody else) and went to Elektra. If they thought that moving to a bigger label would break them worldwide they were in for some disillusionment. Their first record for the company was remixed by Larry Levan. Larry was more of a disco than hip hop mixer, known for records such as Instant Funk's 'I Got My Mind Made Up' or Skyy's 'First Time Around'. For one reason or another, 'Just Rock' (based on Gary Numan's 'Cars') was a flop.

ROCKIN' IT: THE FEARLESS FOUR AT THE FUNHOUSE

The Fearless Four feel that the most commercial rap comes from the ideas of the rappers and DJs themselves. As soon as the company feels it knows best then the records lose their street appeal. They claim 'Just Rock' as the first punk-rock rap (an unholy alliance if ever there was one). Their friends, The Cold Crush Brothers, added to the new genre with 'Punk Rock Rap' on Tuff City Records, a record which combines the renowned Cold Crush rhymes with a self-consciously 'English' feel – icy synthesisers, rock guitar and fake British accents. The notion of punk is so exotic up on Washington Avenue where the Cold Crusher Supreme EZ AD lives that it's no surprise that punk rap turns out to be a hilarious multiple pile-up of heavy metal, synthesiser rock and hip hop. The white boys got their own back with a nasty pornographic scratch record called 'Cookie Puss' on Ratcage. 'Cookie Puss' was by Beastie Boys, a white hardcore group whose favourite band turned out to be Kiss. Inspired by a Mr Carvel soft ice-cream promotion (Cookie Puss – ice-cream sandwich from outer space), it brought together oral sex, telephone violence, food and sexually transmitted diseases as well as an implied racism. Back in the cage, Beastie Boys.

Cold Crush and The Fearless Four may well feel that their rock rap is new but black rock has been around for a long time. Jimi Hendrix and Sly Stone provided models for it, pursued during the '70s by groups like The Jimmy Castor Bunch, Funkadelic, Sons of Slum, War, The Barkays and The Skullsnaps and more recently by Prince and Rick James. Two musicians on the edges of the rap scene worked together in Detroit in

the middle '70s in the crossover area of funk rock. Dennis Weeden, who has worked with Ms DJ, Kenton Nix and Lenny White, came to New York in 1977 with Bill Laswell, a bass player. Weeden and Laswell played together in a group called Solar Eclipse in Michigan and after sharing a loft for a year both branched out in their own directions.

In 1979 Laswell teamed up with synthesiser player Michael Beinhorn, drummer Fred Maher and guitarist Cliff Culteri to form a group called Material – the original core of a floating aggregation of musicians drawn from free jazz, free improvisation and dance music. Through an association with a French-run record label called Celluloid, sited near Times Square, Laswell and Beinhorn came to produce a number of mainly electronic rap records. Bill gives the story:

> It was through this label we have called Celluloid. They were gonna do some records for France. I had heard the music before but I wasn't directly involved in doing tracks like that. We were doing dance tracks which all the kids who were doing these rap records had heard and were playing in clubs and stuff already. It came about as an obligation to a label to produce really quickly five rap records. At the time they were very easy to make 'cos I had already been through the process of making funk records so it was just minimalising and emphasising certain elements more than others. I didn't think the music meant really anything. It was just kinda fun to do. It was more fun to make than it was to listen to.

Of the five records that resulted, one was produced by The Clash, a feeble and amateurish history of graffiti by spray-can artist Futura 2000; The Smurfs' 'Smurf For What It's Worth' involved members of The Peech Boys and is laughably bad; 'Une Sale Histoire' by Fab Five Freddy is dispensable but for its B side featuring Beside, a white woman from California who raps in French; 'The Roxy' by Phase II has a strong minimalism, and 'Grandmixer Cuts It Up' by Grandmixer D.ST and the Infinity Rappers (KC Roc and Shahiem) was deep in video wars – sequencer blips, vocoder vocals, random-fire electric percussion and Smart Bomb blasts. Defender comes to your turntable.

Grandmixer D.ST's favourite video game is Ms Pacman; his favourite TV show is *Star Trek*. The full-colour sleeves for these five Celluloid releases were ikons of the hip-hop scene – graffiti artworks on the back and personality portraits on the front. The Grandmixer (real name Derek Showard, whose home is Delancy Street on the lower east side – hence the D.ST tag) is posing in his room wearing a variant on the b boy uniform complete with white gloves. Behind him are his two turntables, mixer and headphones, coloured vinyl discs and a pair of 3-D glasses. To his right is his TV, his briefcase and his shades. B boying is about being cool.

The weakness of the records is that none of the featured artists was doing anything reflecting his own talents. Fab Five Freddy, Futura and Phase II are graffiti artists and D.ST is a DJ and scratch mixer. Freddy (Braithwaite) is candid about his own role in the scene, upsetting the frequent collusion between the media and hip hop that all b boys and b girls were born in burnt-out tenements. Born in Brooklyn, he admits, 'I was a voyeur at the time hip hop was created but I was a catalyst in bringing it to a wider thing.' His parents were lawyers (his father managed jazz musicians like drummer Max Roach and trumpeter Clifford Brown) and he studied logic in college for a while but moved on to graffiti, making a reputation for himself by spraying the side of an IRT train with his own version of Andy Warhol's silkscreen soup cans. Freddy was a founder member of the Brooklyn graffiti squad, The Fabulous Five, along with Lee Quinones.

With rap being consumed with such voracity by a worldwide audience largely unfamiliar with black music tradition, it is inevitable that distinctions should become blurred. In pop music, stars tend to be represented as images rather than as human beings with specific abilities. Therefore, it's hardly surprising that Afrika Bambaataa, Grandmaster Flash and Fab Five Freddy are regarded as rappers. Only gradually has hip hop come to be seen as an *attitude* which made its mark on forms of expression that had been around for years – dancing, fashion, graffiti, disc jockeying and schoolyard rapping.

Most graffiti artists claim that their movement was started by a teenager tagged

CRAZY CUTS: GRANDMIXER D.ST AT THE EARTH'S EDGE

TAKI 183, a Greek boy named Demetrios from West 183rd Street. TAKI was king of the Magic Markers from 1970 to 1972, yet graffiti was already a subject of study in the '60s. R. Lincoln Keiser's study of the Chicago Vice Lords has numerous photographs of wall writing – territorial markings with club names – and Herbert Kohl's essay, 'Names, Graffiti and Culture', is an analysis of both the reasons behind graffiti and the tags used by artists in place of their legal names. Kohl noted the changes taking place in graffiti as anti-poverty programmes in the late '60s legitimised wall writing by bringing together the youthful black and Puerto Rican artists with socially motivated painters. This sanctioned outdoor art led to more elaborate forms growing out of basic chalk or Magic Marker scribbling. Each borough shouted its identity with a distinct calligraphic style – bubble letters in the Bronx, a Manhattan style, a Queens style and a Brooklyn style called 'Wildstyle'. Artists formed into clubs, an extension of the established neighbourhood gangs – in Brooklyn The Ex(perienced) Vandals, The Vanguards, Magic Inc, The Nod Squad, The A Last Survivors – and bombings upped their daring from nervously scribbled tags into inconceivably detailed wall-size murals or completed trains, painted at night in the yards.

In no other city in the world has vernacular art impinged so fiercely. For a decade and a half the City has been at battle with its teenage art community. Herbert Kohl puts it into perspective: 'Graffiti is not a particularly durable form of expression . . . It is

DOUBLE TROUBLE, CHARLIE AHEARN AND FAB FIVE FREDDY MEET BACKSTAGE AT DANCETERIA

different for the rich and powerful who express their territorial claims and social identities in more durable forms. A gang can paint its name on the walls of its turf, but that is nothing compared to a corporation that stamps its emblem on its buildings or a rich man's club that embodies in stone its claim to power and importance.'

Even more transitory than graffiti are the dance styles that form a part of hip-hop subculture. The south Bronx dance known as Breaking was usurped by the Freak when Chic released 'Le Freak' in 1978, and it was only the intervention of tradition-conscious dancers Crazy Legs (aka Ritchie Colon) and Frosty Freeze (aka Wayne Frost) which kept it alive. Breaking originally concentrated on the legs and feet (bell-bottom trousers pulled up to reveal white socks which showed off steps to advantage in the darkness of the clubs) but Crazy Legs, Frosty Freeze and The Rock Steady Crew added an acrobatic element – worked out in the sandlots of Central Park then moving onto grass and finally concrete – which made Breaking the prime competitive dance as well as giving it a sensational flavour perfect for media fodder.

Through The Rock Steady Crew and countless other dance groups – Incredible Breakers, Electric Force, The Magificent Force, ABC, UTFO – Breaking became a dazzling display of body-punishing spins on the back, shoulders, hands and head. Combined with the west coast invention of Electric Boogie (like electric shock waves jerking through the limbs), Moonwalking (the illusion of gliding across the ground), Joint Popping, Freezes, Mime and Robot Imitations, Breaking became a freestyle dance that actualised all the key imagery of space age, video age, computer age, comic book and superhero America.

According to Afrika Bambaataa, Breaking started as a dance to James Brown's 'Get On the Good Foot':

I said the long hair hippies and the Afro-blacks,
They all get together across the tracks and they party,
Ho – on the good foot.
Ain't nothing going on – but the rent-a,
A whole lotta bills and my money's spent,
And that's on my bad foot.

In a deeply traditional ritual dating back to Southern customs and beyond to West Africa, the dancers would form a circle and take turns to solo in the centre. The word *break* or *breaking* is a music and dance term (as well as a proverb) that goes back a long way. Some tunes, like 'Buck Dancer's Lament' from early this century, featured a two-bar silence in every eight bars for the break – a quick showcase of improvised dance steps. Others used the same device for a solo instrumental break: one of the most fetishised fragments of recorded music is the famous four-bar break taken by Charlie Parker in Dizzy Gillespie's tune 'Night in Tunisia'.

Many of the dance moves used in current freestyle hark back to American dances from the past. In Marshall and Jean Stearns's *Jazz Dance*, Pigmeat Markham recalls the dancing of Jim Green in AG Allen's Mighty Minstrels tent show during

PAPO, MIGUEL AND CHRIS ON THE 6 TRAIN

GRAFFITI ON THE 6 TRAIN

the early 1920s: ' "Green had a speciality I'll never forget. He'd dance awhile and then fall on the floor and spin around on his backside in time with the music." '

Other dancers from vaudeville and minstrel shows had routines that show a mysterious continuity with all the 'new' tricks: a white dancer called Joe Bennett could move across a stage with his body held in a rigid sitting posture; flash dancer (no, that's not a new term, either) Ananias Berry from The Berry Brothers (who worked together from 1925 to 1951) could strut across a stage in a manner described by the authors of *Jazz Dance* as ' "freezing and melting" like frames in a film strip'; Albert

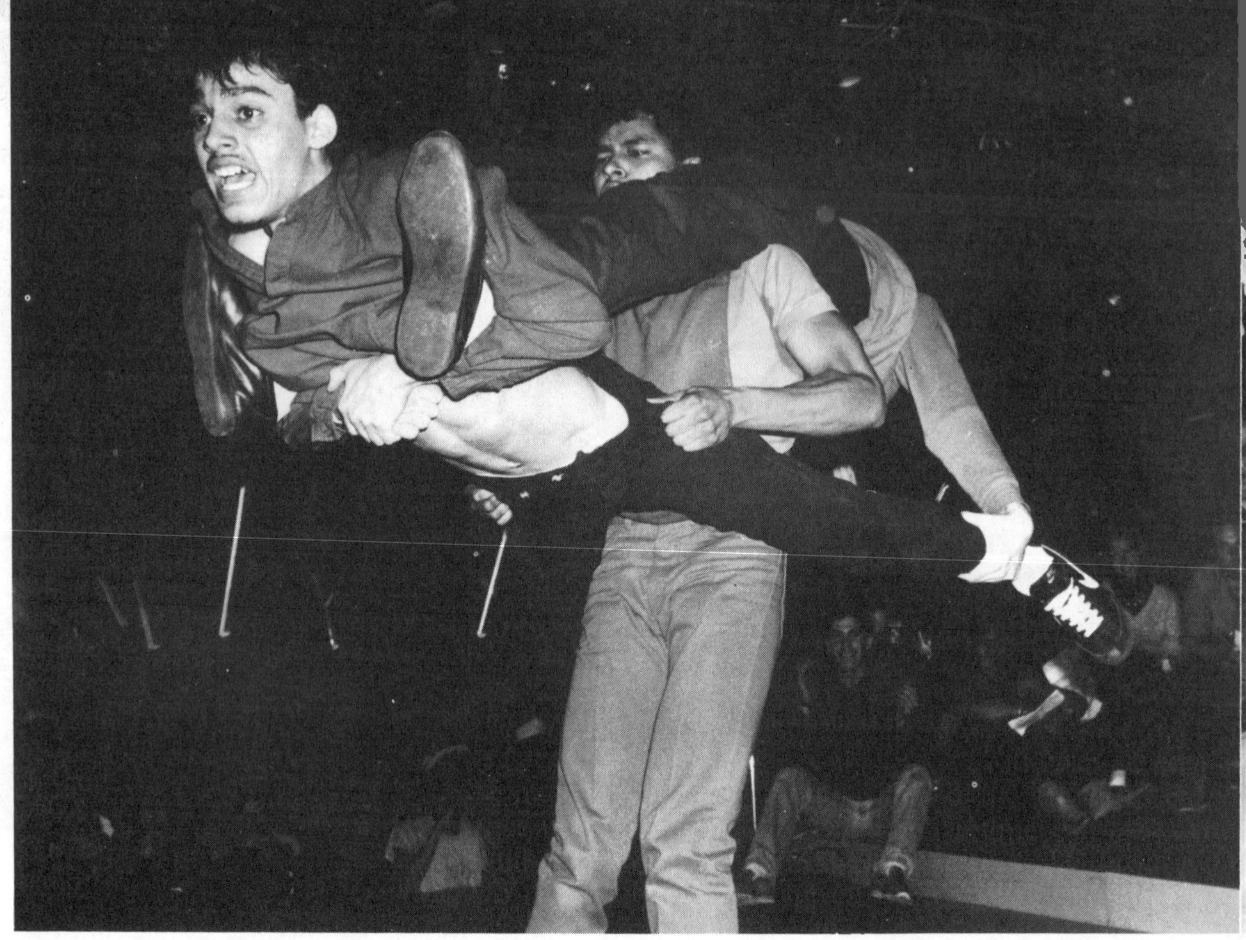

'Pops' Whitman, from Pops and Louis, spun like a top back in the 1940s; Tip Tap and Toe could slide in any direction; Jigsaw Jackson the Human Corkscrew danced with his chin on the Cotton Club stage to the accompaniment of Duke Ellington's Jungle Band. He could also point his face and toes in opposite directions.

Many of the eccentric and comedy dances like Scratch or Itch dancing, Rubberlegs, or Legomania, and Shake dances, also prefigure Breaking and Popping, while the acrobatic element of modern Breaking goes back to before 1900. *Jazz Dance* offers the following comments on early acrobatics: 'The earliest and best-known Negro acrobats were tumblers, who worked *on the ground* performing somersaults, cartwheels, flips and spins . . . Tumbling is geared-to-the-ground, do-it-yourself acrobatics, which anyone can afford. It also lends itself readily to the dance'.

Acrobatics are not just easily applied to dance. They are also extremely dramatic and like all the other forms of hip-hop style they take the most limited resources from an impoverished environment and raise them to extraordinary heights of creativity.

BREAKING THREE-UP AT THE ROXY

YOUNG BREAKERS AT THE ROXY

In the early days, most rappers, dancers, DJs and graffiti artists lost sleep trying to figure new ways of crushing the opposition. Competition was relentless but the invention was high.

The more straightforward steps that didn't lead to concussion, fractured bones and Robbie the Robot tics – the kind of dances that are recycled every decade with new names – were still around. This time they had names like the Patty Duke, the Smurf and the Webo. With the latter two came a music that took the final warp out into hyperspace.

11. Wotupski, bug byte?

'Planet Rock' was like a light being switched on. The black music charts of 1982 were peppered with electronic records – space-breaking releases included Planet Patrol's 'Play At Your Own Risk', 'Nunk' by Warp 9, Tyrone Brunson's 'The Smurf', 'Message 2 (Survival)' by Melle Mel and Duke Bootee, The Fearless Four's 'Rockin' It', 'Hip Hop Be Bop (Don't Stop)' by Man Parrish, George Clinton's *Computer Games* album, 'Scorpio' by Grandmaster Flash and the Furious Five, 'Pack Jam' by The Jonzun Crew, and Whodini's 'Magic's Wand'. Although these records were parallel with the electronic soul of D Train, Kashif, The Peech Boys and The System or the late Patrick Cowley's hi-energy production for Sylvester (derived from Giorgio Moroder's sequencer disco), they differed in being militantly juvenile. Pop culture is inspirational and electro is craze music, a soundtrack for vidkids to live out fantasies born of a science-fiction revival (courtesy of *Star Wars* and *Close Encounters of the Third Kind*) and a video games onslaught.

Nobody can play Defender or Galaxian for long without being affected by those sounds – sickening rumbles and throbs, fuzzy explosions and mindless melodies – and when Gorf and Gorgar began to talk, the whole interactive games phenomenon took on a menacing aspect. Do they know that you've just spent all your mother's money? Do they care that your fantasies are

CHILLING OUT AT THE FUNHOUSE

Bally
PARAGON

saturated with deep blue space wars and glowing violet electronic insects? All the electro boogie records that flew in the 'Planet Rock' slipstream used a variant on imagery drawn from computer games, video, cartoons, sci-fi and hip-hop slanguage. Just as The Cuff Links defined boy/girl relationships through nuclear war images in their doo-wop ballad 'Guided Missiles' (recorded in the A-bomb-conscious 1950s), so Warp 9 sang 'Girl, you're looking good on my video' in the Casio keyboard-powered 'Nunk' (a hybrid of New wave and fUNK).

The whole electro genre fell under the appellation of hip hop, even if it was only distantly related to original Bronx style. Saturday morning TV cartoons were a rich source for b boy/girl source material. The Smurf, for example, was a dance named after the Hanna-Barbera cartoons developed from an adaptation of characters in an early '60s French comic called *Spiro*. The Smurfs had a fetching slang – very hip hop – which substituted verbs, as in 'My potion is wearing off. We'd better smurf out of here.' Washington-born bass player Tyrone Brunson made a record called 'The Smurf' which was pure dance-craze instrumental. It outraged the Smurf copyright holders. Dance discs that followed included 'Letzmurph Acrossdasurf' by the Micronawts (The Micronauts were Marvel Comics' 'heroes minute in size . . . but mighty beyond measure' who came from a sub-atomic solar system called the *Microverse*). On this Tuff City release, dub-mixed by Afrika Bambaataa, they were the alter ego of *Village Voice* music critic Barry Michael Cooper. Since Micronauts, like Smurfs, are very small they have squeaky voices – a fact seized upon by critics of the electro genre as a sign of weakness and a throwback to David Seville's Chipmunks. They forget that dance music has always had a fondness for small creatures with high voices: the parents of The Micronawts were The Chubukos, who in 1973 recorded their tribute to Seville's 1958 US number one, 'Witch Doctor', with a thinly disguised version of Manu Dibango's 'Soul Makossa' called 'Witch Doctor Bump'. Another smurf record was 'Salsa Smurf' by Special Request – a collaboration on Tommy Boy between two contributors to NYC radio station 92KTU, Carlos DeJesus and Jose 'Animal' Diaz. Diaz also mixed Rhetta Hughes's electro hi-energy 'Angel Man', a paean to the subway Guardian Angels, and the Jonzun Crew's 'We Are the Jonzun Crew'. There was also 'Smerphies Dance' on Telestar Cassettes by Spyder D, a young man named Duane Hughes who produced the nightmarishly claustrophobic 'Get Into the Mix' by DJ Divine.

'Get Into the Mix' was inspired by the soundtrack of an Italian porno movie called *How Funny Can Sex Be* and its theme, 'Sesso Matto', released on West End Records. Like *Cooley High* and *Willie Dynamite*, *How Funny Can Sex Be* was a soundtrack with beats that could be cut by DJs. 'Get Into the Mix', along with a very few other records, was a new sub-genre of hip hop pornography.

Another dance craze of the period, along with the Smurf, was the Webo or Huevo (Spanish for egg). It, too, had its very own audiotrack, typical of '82–'83 madhouse dub mixes. Called 'Huevo Dancing' and released on Catawba, it was a creation of veteran soul producer George Kerr and keyboardist/guitarist Reggie Griffin. Its Latino/black soap opera intro, violent electric drums and seemingly random attacks on the mixing-desk faders made it the perfect illustration of the direction dance music was taking. Both Kerr and Griffin were associated with the Sylvia and Joe Robinson empire, and Reggie Griffin went on to make his own electro boogie record, 'Mirda Rock', for Sweet Mountain Records, a Sugarhill subsidiary.

Also doing some uncredited session work at Sugarhill was a Florida-born multi-instrumentalist named Michael Johnson, the periwigged force behind The Jonzun Crew. The Jonzun Crew mixed electronic drums, keyboards and vocoders with an image based on a black composer who gave proto multi-media concerts in Europe in the eighteenth century. 'Pack Jam' (originally called 'Pac Man' and released on the Johnson Brothers' own label, Boston International) was a video-game record, take it or leave it. Like 'Mirda Rock ('I am a computer') or Tilt's 'Arkade Funk' ('I am an arcade funk machine') there was no beating about the bush. These records were an invitation for kids to plunge themselves Tron-like into a world of freeze-frame See Threepios, and if adults wanted to run scared then that was their business – it was the reality of new technology that they were running from.

Many of the electro musicians and producers recognise their music as the fusion that it is – street funk and hip hop mixed with influences from British synthesiser music (Gary Numan, Human League, Thomas Dolby and Yazoo were all played on WKTU, the radio station that switched from rock to disco in 1978, and on WBLS by Frankie Crocker), Latin music, Kraftwerk and jazz fusion, all written into the breaker, robot, pop, wave and moonwalk meltdown. The music of Miles Davis and Herbie Hancock was an important antecedent. Davis's *Filles De Kilimanjaro* is a cool, infinitely subtle pre-echo of electro, and his *Bitches Brew* and *On the Corner*, along with Herbie Hancock's *Headhunters*, gave currency to the image of tribal Africa combined with state-of-the-art electronics. Hancock even stole a touch of rain-forest pygmy music (the polyphonic alternation of vocal yodelling and one-note whistle) for the intro of his 'Watermelon Man' remake. This was exactly a decade before the *Future Shock* album with its hit single 'Rockit'. 'Rockit' was a Material production obliquely inspired by *Headhunters*. In among the Fairlight, Chroma, Emulator and alphaSyntauri, the bata drums and the DMX, the Led Zeppelin guitar chord and the Vocoder, Grandmixer D.ST is featured cutting in rhythmic fills with turntable scratching of a record of the Ketjak Balinese Monkey dance. *Plus ça change*.

All music has a history, shameful or illustrious, but for a 14-year-old chilling out in Playland, white nylon anorak with the hood pulled tight and maybe a pair of Nike kicks with the tongues stuck out, what matters in the mini-phones plugged into the Walkman (or one of its cheaper variants) is the post - NASA - Silicone Valley - Atari - TV Break Out - Taito - Sony - Roland - Linn - Oberheim - Lucas - Speilberg groove. With his use of the Fairlight, a (very expensive) microcomputer system which samples sounds that can be used musically by means of either a keyboard or a light pen acting directly on a VDU, the English producer Trevor Horn has sidestepped the issue of having worked in the desperately unhip Buggles and Yes and gone straight to the hearts of the Bronx techno-warriors.

Lotti Golden and Richard Scher, Warp 9 producers, are equally unlikely as progenitors of the new-wave funk but their commitment to a medium generally considered junk food is disarming. Warp 9 are the perfect instance of hip hop's contemporary ramifications. Their second record, 'Light Years Away', was a 'when gods were space-people' sci-fi tale of alien visitation partially inspired by 'The Message'. It was created by a team which typifies current music-making: two percussionist/singers – Boe Brown who worked with The Strikers, and Chuck Wansley previously of The Charades; singer Ada Dyer who went on to work in the stage show of *The Wiz*; mixer and Funhouse DJ Jellybean; producer and ex-jazz fusion keyboard player Richard Scher, and producer/lyricist/vocalist Lotti Golden. Lotti explains her background:

> I was an artist first. I had a record on Atlantic Records a while ago (1969) and it was a street record of its time. It was called 'Motorcycle'. Stream-of-consciousness rapping, singing about life in New York. It's a collector's item – you can still get it. And then I drifted into jazz for a while. I was very fascinated by jazz. I wanted to sing jazz because to me that was the epitome . . . then starting in the late '70s back to writing R&B. Years ago, Patti LaBelle and the Bluebelles recorded one of my songs. You never heard of it! It was called 'Dance To the Rhythm of Love'. It was a big hit in the Bahamas.
>
> I've been doing music for a real long time and I do what I wanna do at the time that I wanna do it. I stay with what I believe in and I really believe in what Richard and I are doing.

WARP 9 AND LOTTI GOLDEN: THE 'BEAT WAVE' PLAYBACK

The big start to their partnership came with writing 'I Specialise In Love' for Sharon Brown on Profile Records. Since then they have produced other electro hip-hop records with similar gorgeous textures and multiple layers to those of the Warp 9 productions – Chilltown's 'Rock the Beat' and 'Girl's Night Out' by Ladies Choice among them.

With the musicality of their productions they make a markedly different kind of electro boogie from the austere and increasingly freakish end of the genre occupied by Run-D.M.C., The B Boys, DJ Divine, The Beat Box Boys, The Boogie Boys, The Disco Four, Pumpkin, Captain Rock and Davy DMX. Focused down hard on the beats, these records are a black metal music for the '80s – a hard-edge ugly/beauty trance as desperate and stimulating as New York itself.

Davy DMX lives in Queens Village. His basement is crammed with electric keyboards, a drum kit, timbales, guitar, twin turntables, tape machines, records, photographs of his family and the ubiquitous Oberheim DMX. All of it is the reward for a spell as DJ with Kurtis Blow, an association which ended with a degree of bitterness on both sides. Originally a guitarist, Davy – whose real name is David Reeves – started in a group called Rhythm and Creation at the age of 16. He explains how economics affected his attitude to music-making:

> If you have a group of eight people in a band – it was hard to get work, you know? If you did get work it wasn't for a lot of money . . . When the DJ thing came out you can get the same money – you can just bring turntables and speakers and take the place of a band. I DJed for about two years. I used to go to the Bronx a lot and see people scratching. We didn't call it scratching. We called it cutting and mixing.
>
> I was the first DJ in Queens to do the quick mixing and stuff like that – cut turntable to turntable real fast and to play beats. They didn't like it at first – there wasn't no words, no melody into it. It was just drums. I played drums for hours with records . . . I was too young

JUNO-60
Roland
OB-8

> to play clubs – I had to go mobile and just play anywhere I could – neighbourhood bebop clubs. I had a DJ organisation called Solar Sound – we never made a record or nothing, it broke up before the record scene started because I was working with Kurtis Blow. Worked with him for five years.

As well as DJing for Kurtis, Davy played guitar in Orange Krush, playing beats-based music with bassist and co-writer Larry Smith and drummer Trevor Gale. Both Davy DMX's first solo release, 'One For the Treble (Fresh)' on Tuff City, and the reconstituted Orange Krush productions for Profile group Run-D.M.C. reflect the new sound – like an electronic update of Mississippi fife and drum music fed into a breaker's yard.

In Run-D.M.C. Joseph Simmons is Run and Darrel McDaniels is D.M.C. Their records, 'It's Like That', 'Sucker MCs' (one of the biggest rap records of 1983), 'Hard Times' and 'Wake Up', are direct-to-disc wall poems rapped in a doggerel style over an unwavering piston beat. The minimal embellishments are restricted to a few rhythmic keyboard stabs or a bass tied in with the kick drum, sound effects and scratch sounds. Despite its initially bleak surface the music employs a cunning use of hooks – its danceability, wit and overall optimism distinguish it from the despair school of rock.

The concurrent fashionability of scratch mixing and sampling keyboards like the Emulator and Fairlight has led to creative pillage on a grand scale and caused a crisis for pre-computer-age concepts of artistic property. The B Boys' 'Cuttin' Herbie' on Vintertainment makes kamikaze raids on Herbie Hancock's 'Rockit', Howard Johnson's 'So Fine' and a voice that could be James Brown. The Beat Box Boys scrape beats from a screaming rock guitar for 'Punch'. The concept of the pop hook – a musical phrase that sticks in the mind – is pared down to a single noise that flashes up like an English word in Japanese script. The Imperial Brothers use a cough on their 'We Come To Rock' and The Boogie Boys use a Tarzan yell, a cuica, a single word – 'certainly' (pronounced New York style 'soyt'n'ley' – some 'classical' music, some 'heavy metal', mixed kitchen-sink method for their exhumation of the rap obsession with astrology, 'Zodiac/Break Dancer/Shake and Break'. The Awesome Foursome use the Tarzan yell for 'Funky Breakdown', and the classical music returns for The Beat Box Boys' 'Give Me My Money'. What next – Beethoven's Fifth? Soyt'n'ley – here comes Vincent Davies's Vintertainment label with 'Beethoven's Fifth Street Symphony'! The stick-up kids are on the loose.

To phone Tommy Boy Records in February '84 was a treat. For as long as you were kept on hold there was the legendary 'Payoff Mix' in your ear – the double D and Steinski mastermix of G.L.O.B.E. and Whiz Kid's 'Play That Beat Mr. D.J.', taking hip-hop cutting one step further into the realm of endless potential. It used the irresistible base of 'Play That Beat' to cut in fragments of 'Adventures On the Wheels of Steel', some James Brown soul power, 'Buffalo Gals', Funky Four's 'That's the Joint', West Street Mob, The Supreme Team, Culture Club, Starski's 'Live At the Disco Fever', Little Richard's 'Tutti Frutti', exercise routines (heel-toe, heel-toe), Humphrey Bogart in *Casablanca*, 'Rockit', The Supremes' 'Stop In the Name of Love', 'Planet Rock', Indeep's 'Last Night a DJ Saved My Life' and more. Like a long subway ride with the doors opening onto a different kind of music at every stop, it perfectly expressed the spirit of G.L.O.B.E.'s words:

Punk rock, new wave and soul
Pop music, salsa, rock & roll
Calypso, reggae, rhythm & blues
Master mix those number one tunes

Hip hop was the new music by virtue of its finding a way to absorb all other music. I.R.T. (Interboro Rhythm Team) sum up the New York mix with their subterranean journey across the city. At Times Square Julio is Breaking to his radio. The beats are electro boogie, the music is a classy salsa montuno from the piano, the dogs are barking, the words are the rap attack. 'Watch the Closing Doors!'

HARD TIMES: RUN - D.M.C.

WATCH THE CLOSING DOORS

Words up!

Compiled and introduced by Monica Lynch from Tommy Boy Records

'Kids say the darndest things!' The advent of electronic hip-hop music during 1982 has brought attention to a very amusing subculture of urban teenagers who have not only galvanised the dance-music industry but who have also created their own clothing, dance and word fashions. The colourful vocabulary you're likely to hear bandied about the Funhouse, Disco Fever and the Roxy demands a lexicon of current street lingo if you're to adopt these expressions and employ them with any authority and the proper inflections. Okay now, with relish:

smurf: a dance named after the Smurf cartoon characters on Saturday morning TV. *Example*: 'Yeah man, that record 'Pack Jam' is great for smurfin' it up.'

def: an adjective used to describe anything that is unquestionably cool. *Example*: 'Animal's mix of 'Planet Rock' and 'Play At Your Own risk' is def.' Animal is a New York DJ noted for his prowess at the turntables, also known as 'the wheels of steel'.

homeboy: a close friend or someone you grew up with. *Example*: 'Jazzy Jay's one of my homeboys. We both was livin' in Co-op City when we was kids.'

whacked: bogus, off the mark, unconvincing or poorly executed. *Example*: 'The rap on that new record is whacked.'

Breakout, dip, or *buff*: all are terms for leaving. *Example*: 'Fellas I'm gonna breakout because I have to meet my woman.'

bitty: female. *Example*: 'Are there going to be a lot of bitties at the party?'

on the jock: a term used by boys to describe girls who are seeking their undivided attention, much to their annoyance. *Example*: 'Man, you know that girl Evie? She's been on my jock all week.'

crash: to hit or cause bodily harm. *Example*: 'If you keep messing with my car, I'm gonna crash you.'

cap: to shoot with a gun. *Example*: 'Did you hear that Frankie got capped at Harlem World last week?'

treacherous or treach: an adjective that means nice or 'on', and definitely has a positive connotation. *Example*: 'That new rap by Soul Sonic Force is positively treach!' There is also a New York-based rap group called The Treacherous Three.

Hook up: to pay back or compensate, usually used in reference to money. *Example*: 'Yo bro', lend me $10 and I'll hook you up on Monday.'

gusto: money, cold cash, dinero. *Example*: 'Hey man, it's Monday. Where's my gusto?'

fresh: an adjective used to describe something, usually clothes, that are good-looking, stylish or cool. *Example*: 'That new gear my man was wearing was fresh!'

word up or *word*: an expression used to signify agreement or understanding. *Example*: Mikey T – 'I just saw *Horror*

Planet. It was a treach flick.' Freeze – 'Word man, I saw it last week.'

kicks: synonymous with sneakers, which are the last word in footwear. Pumas and Nikes are the current favourites. *Example*: 'I gotta get me some new kicks to wear to the Funhouse Saturday,' The Funhouse, by the way, is a popular disco with this crowd.

shank: to stab with a knife or any other sharp object. *Example*: 'I'm gonna shank that bastard if he doesn't chill fast.'

zooted: to be drunk, high, etc. *Example*: 'That smoke got me zooted quick.'

chill: to relax or cool out. *Example*: 'Take a chill pill Moms. All the guys are into hangin' on the Deuce.' 'Chilling out' is also popular.

chilly most: the ultimate of relaxation. *Example*: 'How you doin' man?' 'I'm chilly most.'

chilling hard: well on your way to frozen. *Example*: 'After five weeks in the House of D, I'm ready to chill hard.' 'House of D' is slang for the House of Detention.

juice: power. *Example*: 'WBLS, the station with juice!' or 'Frankie's got a fresh image but Carlos got juice.'

crew: a group of guys who hang out together. *Example*: 'Me and my crew were at the Zulu Nation Anniversary party last week.'

maxin' and relaxin': same as 'chilling out'.

down by law: used to describe someone who is a veteran or an expert at something, or to describe their work. *Example*: 'When it comes to rap attacks, Mr Magic's down by law'. Mr Magic is a popular New York air personality.

Deuce: Forty-Second Street or the Times Square area. *Example*: 'Those drugs I got on the Deuce are whacked.'

tipsters: groupies. *Example*: 'Those kids hanging around WBLS are Magic's tipsters.'

Gunsmoke: Brooklyn.

Do Or Die: Bedford-Stuyvesant housing centre.

Chill Town: Jersey City.

Boogie Down Bronx: The Bronx.

Money Makin' Manhattan: self-explanatory.

rap attack: a quick-paced onslaught of 'def' expressions delivered with stylish verbal dexterity.

Lightning swords of death

One Hundred Rap Attacks: these are all 12-inch singles with their American labels given in preference to those of the British releases. Some of them are in the list for historical importance, others because I like them. Strictly *not* in order of preference.

1. Afrika Bambaataa, 'Death Mix' (Winley)
2. Afrika Bambaataa and Cosmic Force, 'Zulu Nation Throwdown' (Winley)
3. Afrika Bambaataa and the Soul Sonic Force, 'Looking For the Perfect Beat' (Tommy Boy)
4. Afrika Bambaataa and the Soul Sonic Force, 'Planet Rock' (Tommy Boy)
5. Afrika Bambaataa and the Soul Sonic Force, 'Renegades of Funk' (Tommy Boy)
6. Beastie Boys, 'Cookie Puss' (Rat-cage)
7. Beat Box Boys, 'Give Me My Money', 'Einstein', 'Yum Yum-Eat 'Em Up' (Memo)
8. Bobby Gilliom, 'Give Me a Break' (Clappers)
9. Bon Rock and Cotton Candy, 'Junior Wants to Play' (Tommy Boy)
10. Bon Rock and the Rhythem Rebellion, 'Searchin' Rap' (Reelin' and Rockin')
11. Brother D, 'How We Gonna Make the Black Nation Rise' (Clappers)
12. Captain Rapp, 'Bad Times (I Can't Stand It)' (Becket)
13. Captain Rock, 'Cosmic Glide' (Nia)
14. Captain Sky, 'Soap Opera City' (Jamtu)
15. CC Crew, 'CC Crew Rap' (Golden Flamingo)
16. Community People, 'Education Wrap' (Delmar International Inc.)
17. Count Coolout, 'Here to Stay (Me and My Double R.R.)' (WMOT)
18. Crash Crew, 'Breaking Bells (Take Me To the Mardi Gras)' (Sugarhill)
19. Davy DMX, 'One For the Treble (Fresh)' (Tuff City)
20. Dimples D. 'Sucker DJs (I Will Survive)' (Party Time)
21. Disco Four, 'Whip Rap' (Profile)
22. DJ Divine, 'Get Into the Mix' (West End)
23. Dr Jeckyl and Mr Hyde, 'Genius Rap' (Profile)
24. Fab Five Freddy 'Une Sale Histoire' (Celluloid)
25. Fantasy 3, 'Biters In the city' (CCL)
26. Fatback Band, 'King Tim III (Personality Jock)' (Spring)
27. Fresh Face, 'Huevo Dancing' (Catawba)
28. Fresh 3 M.C.s, 'Fresh' (Profile)
29. Funky Four Plus One, 'That's The Joint' (Sugarhill)
30. Funky Four Plus One More, 'Rappin' and Rockin' the House' (Enjoy)
31. Gary Byrd and the G.B. Experience, 'The Crown' (Motown)
32. George Clinton, 'Nubian Nut' (Capitol)
33. G.L.O.B.E. and Whiz Kid, 'Play That Beat Mr D.J.' (Tommy Boy)

34. Grandmaster and Melle Mel, 'Jesse' (Sugarhill)
35. Grandmaster Flash, 'Adventures of Grandmaster Flash on the Wheels of Steel' (Sugarhill)
36. Grandmaster Flash and the Furious Five, 'Flash To the Beat' (Bozo Meko bootleg)
37. Grandmaster Flash and the Furious Five, 'Flash To the Beat' (Sugarhill)
38. Grandmaster Flash and the Furious Five, 'Superrappin'' (Enjoy)
39. Grandmaster Flash and the Furious Five, 'The Message' (Sugarhill)
40. Grandmixer D.ST, 'Crazy Cuts' (Island)
41. Grandmixer D.ST and the Infinity Rappers, 'Grandmixer Cuts It Up' (Celluloid)
42. Hurt 'Em Bad and the S.C. Band, 'Martin Luther' (Profile)
43. Hurt 'Em Bad and the S.C. Band, 'The Boxing Game' (Profile)
44. I.R.T., 'Watch the Closing Doors' (RCA)
45. Jazzy Five/Kryptic Krew, 'Jazzy Sensation' (Tommy Boy)
46. King Tim III, 'Charlie Says (Roller Boogie Baby)' (Spring)
47. K9 Corp featuring Pretty C, 'Dog Talk' (Capitol)
48. Kurtis Blow, 'Party Time' (Mercury)
49. Kurtis Blow, 'The Breaks' (Mercury)
50. Lady B, 'To the Beat Y'All' (Tec)
51. Lady D, 'Lady D' (Reflection)
52. Love Bug Starski, 'You've Gotta Believe' (The Fever)
53. Malcolm X/Keith LeBlanc, 'No Sell Out' (Tommy Boy)
54. Men at Play, 'Dr Jam (In the Slam)' (Sunshine)
55. Nairobi, 'Soul Makossa Rap' (Streetwise)
56. Naomi Peterson, 'Sweet Naomi Rap' (Heavenly Star)
57. Nice and Nasty Three, 'The Ultimate Rap' (Holiday)
58. Paulette and Tanya Winley, 'Rhymin' and Rappin'' (Winley)
59. Pee Wee Mel and Barry B, 'Life On the Planet Earth' (12 Star)
60. Phase II, 'The Roxy' (Celluloid)
61. Planet Patrol, 'Play At Your Own Risk' (Tommy Boy)
62. Pumpkin, 'King Of the Beat' (Profile)
63. Rammelzee Vs. K-Rob, 'Beat Bop' (Profile)
64. Reggie Griffen and Techno Rock, 'Mirda Rock' (Sweet Mountain)
65. Rockers Revenge, 'Sunshine, Partytime Rap' (Streetwise)
66. Rock Master Scott and the Dynamic 3, 'It's Life (You Gotta Think Twice)' (Profile)
67. Ronnie Gee, 'Raptivity' (Reflection)
68. Sequence, 'Funk You Up' (Sugarhill)
69. Shango, 'Shango Message' (Celluloid)
70. She, 'Ms D.J. Rap It Up!' (Clappers)
71. Slim, 'It's In the Mix' (D.E.T.T.)
72 .South Bronx, 'The Bottom Line' (Rissa Chrissa)
73. Special Request, 'Salsa Smurf' (Tommy Boy)
74. Spoonie Gee, 'Spoon'nin' Rap' (Sugarhill)
75. Spoonie Gee, 'The Big Beat' (Tuff City)
76. Spoonie Gee/The Treacherous

Three, 'The New Rap Language'/ 'Love Rap' (Enjoy)

77. Spyder-D, 'Smerphies Dance' (Telestar Cassettes)
78. Sugarhill Gang, 'Rapper's Delight' (Sugarhill)
79. Sula, 'Jungle Rap' (Starwave)
80. Sweet G, 'A Heartbeat Rap' (West End)
81. Tanya Sweet Tee Winley, 'Vicious Rap' (Winley)
82. The B Boys, 'Two, Three Break' (Vintertainment)
83. The Beat Boys, 'Be Bop Rock' (Sugarscoop)
84. The Boogie Boys, 'Zodiac/Break Dancer/Shake and Break' (Capitol)
85. The Cold Crush Brothers, 'Punk Rock Rap' (Tuff City)
86. The Disco Four, 'Country Rock Rap' (Enjoy)
87. The Fearless Four, 'Problems of the World' (Elektra)
88. The Fearless Four, 'Rockin' It' (Enjoy)
89. The Force MDs, 'Let Me Love You' (Tommy Boy)
90. The Last Poets, 'Long Enough' (Kee Wee)
91. The Rake, 'Street Justice' (Profile)
92. The Treacherous Three, 'Feel the Heartbeat' (Enjoy)
93. The Younger Generation, 'We Rap More Mellow' (Brass)
94. Tilt, 'Arkade Funk' (D.E.T.T.)
95. Time Zone, 'Wildstyle' (Celluloid)
96. Trickeration, 'Rap Bounce Rockskate' (Sound of New York)
97. Trouble Funk, 'Pump Me Up' (Jam)
98. T Ski Valley, 'Catch the Beat' (Grand Groove)
99. Wayne and Charlie 'Check It Out' (Sugarhill)
100. Whodini, 'Magic's Wand' (Jive)

The following albums are also recommended (even though rap is music for 12-inch singles):
Run-D.M.C. (Profile), *Crash Crew Meets Funky Four* (Sugarhill/Vogue, French LP), Warp 9 *It's a Beat Wave* (Prism), *Wildstyle* (Animal Records soundtrack LP), Jonzun Crew *Lost In Space* (21 Records/ Tommy Boy), *Genius of Rap* (Island UK Sampler), *The Perfect Beat* (Tommy Boy/Polydor UK sampler), *Live Convention '82*, Vols 1 & 2 (Soul On Wax), *Rapped Uptight*, Vols 1 & 2 (Sugarhill/PRT UK samplers), *Electro*, Vol 1 onwards (Street Sounds UK samplers), *The Big Break Rapper Party*, Vol 1 (Sound of New York, USA/Queen Constance), Grandmaster Flash and the Furious Five *The Message* (Sugarhill), *Enjoy* (New York Connexion UK sampler), *Super Disco Brakes*, Vols 1 to 4 (Winley).

Bibliography

Books

Abrahams, Roger D., *Deep Down In the Jungle*, second edition, New York: Aldine 1970.

Ali, Muhammad, *The Greatest*, England: Mayflower 1976.

Anderson, Jervis, *Harlem: The Great Black Way*, London: Orbis 1982.

Brown, H. Rap, *Die Nigger, Die!*, New York: Dial Press 1961.

Courlander, Harold, *Negro Folk Music USA*, New York: Columbia University Press 1963

Cripps, Thomas, *Black Film As Genre*, Bloomington and London: Indiana University Press 1979

Finnegan, Ruth, *Oral Literature In Africa*, Oxford: Oxford University Press 1970.

Fox, Ted, *Showtime At the Apollo*, New York: Holt Rinehart & Winston 1983.

Gillespie, Dizzy, with Fraser, Al, *Dizzy – To Be Or Not to Bop*, London: Quartet 1979.

Groia, Philip, *They All Sang On the Corner*, second edition, New York: Phillie Dee Enterprises Inc 1983.

Heilbut, Tony, *The Gospel Sound*, New York: Anchor/Doubleday 1975.

Jackson, Bruce, *Wake Up Dead Man*, Cambridge Massachusetts: Harvard University Press 1972.

Kochman, Thomas, *Rappin' and Stylin' Out*, Chicago: University of Chicago Press 1977.

Kohl, Herbert, and Hinton, James, 'Names, Graffiti, and Culture', (printed in *Rappin' and Stylin' Out*, see above.)

Kurlansky, Mervyn; Naar, Jon; and Mailer, Norman, *Watching My Name Go By*, Matthews Miller Dunbar, no date.

Keiser, R. Lincoln, *The Vice Lords*, New York: Holt Rinehart & Winston 1969.

Labov, William, 'Rules for Ritual Insults', (printed in *Rappin' and Stylin' Out*, see above.)

Oliver, Paul, *Savannah Syncopators*, London: Studio Vista 1970.

Sterns, Marshall and Jean, *Jazz Dance*, New York: Schirmer 1979.

Roberts, John Storm, *Black Music of Two Worlds*, New York: Praeger 1972.

Magazines

Blues Unlimited, No. 129, London, 1978.

Right On! Focus Rap Musical Special, New Jersey, D.S. Magazines 1983.

Wavelength: New Orleans Music Magazine, Issue 37, New Orleans 1983.

As co-editor of *Collusion* magazine I've had the opportunity to be involved with many articles that proved to be sources of inspiration and ideas for this book – in particular, articles by Stuart Cosgrove, Matthew Wright, Nick Kimberley, Barbara Peterson, Steven Harvey, Jeb Nichols and my co-editors, Sue Steward and Steve Beresford.' *Collusion* issues 1 to 5 are available from 14 Peto Place, London NW1.

Index

Please note: due to the frequency of tags or nicknames in this book all names are alphabeticised by the first name rather than the family name.

Page numbers in italics refer to photographs.

Aaron Fuchs, 92, *119*, 119–20
Abbey Lincoln, 118
African Music Machine, 42
Afrika Bambaataa, 8, *19*, 19, 39, *57*, 56–60, 65–6, 69, 97, 99, 104, 105, 115, 120, 125, 126, *131*, 129–33, 142, 148
Alan Lomax, 28
All Platinum Records, 79, 86, 105
Alvin Cash, 42
Angie B, 95
Ann Winley, 93
Apollo Theatre, 39, 69, 83, 88
Archie Shepp, 118
Arthur Baker, *108*, 108–110, *131*, 131
Audubon Ballroom, 24, 74–6, 112

Babatunde Olatunji, 42
Babe Ruth, 131
Babs Gonzalez, 18, 38
Baby D, 93–4
Baby Huey and the Babysitters, 67
The Back Door, 72–4
Barbara Mason, 17, 52
Barry White, 41, 47, 51, 60, 62, 93
B Boys, 151, 153
Beastie Boys, 137
Beat Box Boys, 151, 153
Beat Street, 36, 56, 134
Beny Moré, 12
Betty Carter, 36
Betty Wright, 52
Big Maybelle, 100, 115
Big Youth, 39, 104
Bill 'Bojangles' Robinson, 22, 36
Bill Laswell, 139
Billy Eckstine, 37
Billy Squier, 67
Black Panthers, 118
Black Spades, 57
Blondie, 95–6
Blowfly, 34
Bo Diddley, 8, 19, *34*, 34, 79
Bob James, 17, 73, 114, 136
Bobby Byrd, 66
Bobby Robinson, 16, 17, 19, 24, 40, *86*, 82–7, 100, 113, 135
Bobby Womack, 50, 124
Bon Rock, 112
Boogie Boys, 151
Bootsy's Rubber Band, 42
Breakdance, 134
Broadway International, 17
Brother D, 120
B.T. Express, 42
Busy Bee Starski, 71, 100, 124, 154
Butterbeans and Susie, 31, 115

Cab Calloway, 19, 36–7
Cameo, 52
Captain Rapp, 124
Captain Rock, 44, 151
Captain Sky, *44*, 44, 114, 130
Carla Thomas, 115
Cassius Clay *see* Muhammad Ali
CC Crew, 29, 95
Celluloid Records, 139
Chakachas, 42
Channels, 84, *86*
Charlie Ahearn, 12, 134, *141*
Charlie Parker, 18, 37, 142
Charts, 84
Cheryl Lynn, 87, 109, 121
Cheryl the Pearl, 95
Chic, 16, 17, 78, 81, 93, 106, 124
Cholly Atkins, 24, 89
Chuck Brown and the Soul Searchers, 42
Clappers Records, 104, 120
Clarence Heyman, 39
Cold Crush Brothers, 81, 113, 137, *138*
Collegians, 98
Community People, 120
Cory Robbins, 110–11
Cosmic Force, 95, 99
Cotton Candy, 108
Cotton Club, 36
Count Basie, 37
Count Machouki, 39
Cowboy, 71–2
Coxsone Dodd, 39
Crash Crew, 114

Daddy 'Jim Crow' Rice, 30
Daddy-O Daylie, 38
Danceteria, 95, 133
Daniel Ponce, 12
Danny Robinson, 16, 100
Dave 'Baby' Cortez, 24, 79, 96, 98
Davy DMX, 151–3, *153*
Debbie D, 93
Delfonics, 73
Dennis Alcapone, 39
Dennis Coffey, 67, 114
Dennis Weeden, 107, 121, 139
Disco Fever, 33
Disco Four, 113, 151
Dixie Club, 74
Dizzy Gillespie, 38
DJ Breakout, 88
DJ Divine, 148, 151
DJ Hollywood, 69, 71, 82, 93
Donnie Elbert, 79
Dorothy Norwood, 47
Double D, 153
Double Trouble, 70–71, *80*, 95, 141
Doug Wimbish, 96, 105, 106, 126
Dr Betty Shabazz, 125
Dr Hep Cat, 38
Dr Horse, 50
Dr Jeckyl and Mr Hyde, 44, *111*, 110–11
Dr Jive, 39
Dr Rock, 26
Dr Shock, 27
Duke Ellington, 37
Dyke and the Blazers, 14, 67, 113

East Harlem Bus Stop, 42
Ed Fletcher (Duke Bootee), 105, 120, 123, 146
Eddie Cheeba, 69
Eddie Jefferson, 18, 37
Eddie Kendricks, 60
Eddie Murphy, 40
Eddie O'Jay, 40
Edna Gallman Cooke, 47
Eek a Mouse, 39
Ella Fitzgerald, 34, 46
Elijah Muhammad, 29
Elivs Presley, 25, 93
Enjoy Records, 16–17, 82–7, 90, 105–7, 113, 135
Ennio Morricone, 130–31
Ernie 'Bubbles' Whitman, 37
Ernie the Whip, 39
Eva Deff, 93
Everlast Records, 84

Fab Five Freddy, 139–40, *141*
Face 2000, 124
Fantastic Aleems, 44, 116
Fatback (or The Fatback Band), 15, 42, 52, 81–2
Fats Waller, 22, 36
Fearless Four, 40, 124, *135*, *137*, 135–7, 146
Flashdance, 22, 134
Flip Wilson, 40, 98
Flowers, 60
Force MDs, *25*, 25–8, *27*
Francis Grasso, 60
Frankie Crocker, 40, 41, 46, 60, 149
Frankie Lymon and the Teenagers, 22–4
Freedom, 105
Funkadelic, 137
Funky Four Plus One More, 8, 71, 80, 87, 90, 95, 106, 114, 133, 154
Furious Five, 8, 33, 47, 67, 90, 105, 116, 120, 123, 126, 146
Futura, 139–40

Garry Byrd, *44*, 44–6
George Clinton, *42*, 42, 44, 146
George Goldner, 24
George Kerr, 50, 79, 99, 149
Georgie Woods, 39
Gil Scott-Heron, 19, 80, 114, 119
Gladys Knight and the Pips, 83, 89
G.L.O.B.E., 131–2, 153–4
Grandmixer D.ST, 12, 107, 139, *140*, 149
Grandmaster Caz, 125
Grandmaster Flash, 8, *16*, 17–18, 26, *61*, 62–5, 67, *74*, 69–78, 80, 88, 90–91, 93, 104–7, 116, 120, *123*, 123, 126, 128, 146
Grand Wizard Theodore, 67, 128
Griots, 8, 19, 31–2
Gwen McCrae, 50

Hamilton Bohannon, 42
Harold Melvin and the Bluenotes, 50
Harry the Hipster Gibson, 37
Herbie Hancock, 12, 17, 136, 149, 153
Helzapoppin', 37
Herculoids, 39
Holiday Records, 16, 100
Honi Coles, 89
H. Rap Brown, 118
Hurt 'Em Bad and the S.C. Band, 124

Imamu Amiri Baraka, 118
Imperial Brothers, 153
Incredible Bongo Band, 60, 73, 114
Irma Thomas, 48, 50
I.R.T., 154
Isaac Hayes, 47, *51*, 51, 69, 98
Isley Brothers, 30, 67, 124

Jack Taylor, 100
Jackie 'Moms' Mabley, 40, 98
Jackson Five (or The Jacksons), 25, 26, 45, 63
Jack the Cat, 38
James Brown, 14, 47, 50, *53*, 53, 58, 63, 66, 93, 98, 99, 113, 118, 120, 142, 153, 154
James P. Johnson, 17, 22
Jazzland Ballroom, 24
Jazzy Five, 108
Jazzy Jay, 56, *57*, 129
JBs, 42, 114
Jerry 'Swamp Dogg' Williams, 48
Jesse Jackson, 124
Jesters, 98
Jiggs Chase, 17, 105, 106
Jigsaw Jackson the Human Corkscrew, 144
Jimi Hendrix, 45, 105, 116, 137
Jimmy Castor, 14, 22–6, *23*, 28, 45, 63, 67, 118, 137
Jimmy Lewis, 50
Jocko Henderson, 24, 39, 42, 113
Joe Bataan, 109–110
Joe Louis, 46
Joe Robinson, 78, 149
Joey Robinson Jr., 81, 114
Joe Tex, *49*, 49
John Blackfoot Colbert, 50
John 'Jellybean' Benitez, 132
John Robie, 131
Johnnie Taylor, 31, 47, *48*
Johnny Otis, 34
Jonzun Crew, 44, 146, 149

Keith LeBlanc, 105, 106, 124
Kenton Nix, 107
King Curtis, 86–7
King Pleasure, 18, 37, 118
King Stitt, 39
King Tim III, 15, *79*, 79, 81–2, 113
KK Rockwell, 71, 81, 88, 94
Kool and the Gang, 42, 119
Kool Dee, 60
Kool DJ AJ, 75
Kool DJ Herc, 18, 39, 60, 62, 63, 65, 69, 104
Kraftwerk, 56, 114, 120, *128*, 130–1, 135, 149
Kryptic Krew, 108
Kurtis Blow, 69, 93, 112, 120, 121, 153

Lady B, 95, 122
Lady D, 95
Langston Hughes, 46
Larry Graham (also Graham Central Station), 127

Last Poets, 19, 105, 114, 116–19
Laura Lee, *48*, 48, 52
Led Zeppelin, 149
Lee Quinones, 140
Lena Horne, 36
Leo Watson, 37
Leslie Uggams, 23
Lil Rodney Cee, 70, 80, 82, 88, 94, 95
Linda Jones, 79
Lisa Lee, 94, 132
Lister Hewan Lowe, 120
Little Johnny Taylor, 50
Lloyd Price, 30
Lolleata Holloway, 52, 81, 108
Lotti Golden, *150*, 150–51
Lou Rawls, 47, 49, 50
Louis Armstrong, 36
Louis Jordan, 17
Luther Ingram, 8, 51

Maboya, 60
Magnificent Seven, 70
Malcolm McLaren, 46, 81, 104, 113, 132
Malcolm X, 29, 46, 58, 97, 118, 124–5, 130
Mandrill, 42, 60
Manu Dibango, 114, 148
Marion Williams, 47
Martin Luther King, 58, 97, 130
Material, 139, 149
Mattie Moultrie, 50
Maurice 'Hotrod' Hulbert, 39
Max Roach, 118
Mel Brooks, 111
Melle Mel (also Melvin Glover), 33, 47, 75, 120, *121*, 123, 124, 128, 146
Melvin Van Peebles, 8, 119
Mercedes Ladies, 93
Meters, 42, 114
Micronawts, 148
Michael Jackson, 25, 56
Mickey 'Guitar' Baker, 17, 78–9
Miles Davis, 149
Milford Graves, 36
Millie Jackson, 47, *51*, 51–3, 98
Minton's Playhouse, 18
Moke and Poke, 31
Moments, 73, 79, 127
Momma Stoppa, 39
Mr Biggs, *59*, 60, 69, 131–2
Mr Magic, 46
Mr T, 25
Ms DJ (also Sheila Spencer), 121, *122*
Muddy Waters, 79
Muhammad Ali, 19, 29, 45, 46, 121

Naomi Peterson, 95
Nation of Islam, 29, 59, 130
New Birth, 67
Nia Records, 44
Nice and Nasty Three, 100
Nipsey Russell, 40, 98

Ohio Players, 42
Okey Dokey, 38
Orange Krush, 153
The Organisation, 59
Orioles, 84
Otis Redding, 83, 115

Paquito D'Rivera, 12
Paragons, 98
Patryce 'Chocolate' Banks, 127
Paul Winley, 16, 17, 19, 24, 67, *97*, 96–100, 113, 124–5
Paulette Winley, 95, 100
Pee Wee Mel and Barry B, 107
Persuasions, 25
Pete DJ Jones, 60, 63
Peter Brown, 92
Phase II, 139–40
Pigmeat Markham, 19, 40, 98, 142
Planet Patrol, 146
Pooche Costello, 91–2
Pow Wow, 131–2
Pressure Drop, 104
Prince, 137
Profile Records, 110–11, 113, 123, 153
Pumpkin, 17, 87–8, 91, 113, 151

Queen Kenya, 60

Rabbit Foot Minstrels, 30
Rainbow Records, 83
The Rake, 123
Rammelzee, 122
Ravens, 84
Ray Scott, 40
Redd Foxx, 34, 40
Reelin' and Rockin' Records, 111–12
Reggie Griffin, 124, 149
Reverend C. L. Franklin, 47
Reverend J. D. Montgomery, 47
Reverend Willie T. Sneed, 47
Rich Cason, 52
Richard Barrett, 24
Richard 'Dimples' Fields, 52
Richard 'Mr Clean' White, 47
Richard Pryor, 8, 40
Richard Scher, 150–51
Rick James, 137
Rockmaster Scott and the Dynamic 3, 124
Rock Steady Crew, 22, 142
Rocky G, 39
Roddy Hui, 93
Rodney Jones, 41
Rojac Records, 100
Rolling Stones, 14
Ronnie Gee, 34
The Roxy, 56, 133
Roy Ayers, 82
Rudy Ray Moore, 34
Rufus Thomas, *30*, 30, 41, 67
Run-D.M.C., 124, 151, 153

Sanctuary, 60
Scoey Mitchlll, 40
Screamin' Jay Hawkins, 40, 123
Sequence, 95, 122
Sha Rock, 87, 94
Shadows, 114
Shakedown Sound, 56
Shango, 42, 56, *131*
Sheila Spencer *see* Ms DJ
Shep Pettibone, 108
Sherry Sheryl, 93
Shirley Brown, 52
Shirley Ellis, 122
Shirley Goodman, 79

Sir Lord Comic, 39
Skullsnaps, 137
Slim Gaillard, 37
Sly Stone (also Sly and the Family Stone), 22, *41*, 41, 63, 67, 126–7, 137
Smokey, 60
Solomon Burke, *49*, 49–50
Sonny Hopson, 39
Sonny Liston, 29
Sons of Slum, 137
Sons of Truth, 50
Soul Children, 50
Soul Sonic Force, 56, 99, *131*, 131–2
Sound of New York USA, 16, 92
South Bronx, 124
Special Request, 148
Speckled Red, 8
Spoonie Gee, 17, *91*, 91–3, 106–7
Spring Records, 15
Spyder D, 148
Steinski, 153
Stevie Wonder, 45, 124, 126
Stormy Weather, 36
Stringbeans and Sweetie May, 115
Sugarhill Gang, 16–17, 76, 78, *79*, 79, 81, 83, 95, 106, 114
Sugarhill Records, 16, 78, 81, 82, 105–6, 124, 126, 149
Sugar Ray Leonard, 47
Sugar Ray Robinson, 38
Sula, 121
Sun Ra, 44, 118
Sweet G, 107
Sweet Tee *see* Tanya Winley
Sylvia Robinson, 16–17, *82*, 78–82, 95, 105–6, 111, 123–4, 126–7, 149
Symphonic B Boys Mixx, 105

Taana Gardner, 56, 107
Taki, 183, 141
Tamberlane, 60
Tami Lynn, 50
Tanya Winley, 95–6, 100, 120
Teddy Pendergrass, 50
Temptations, 45, *89*, 88–90
Thin Lizzy, 14, 67
Tilt, 149
Timmie 'Clark Dark' Rogers, 40
Tina B, 108
Tip Tap and Toe, 144
Tito Puente, 14
Tom Silverman, 56, 108
Tom Tom Club, 110, 134
Tommy Boy Records, 56, 104, 108, 124, 130, 153
Tout Sweet, 52
Treacherous Three, 8, 91, 107
Trevor Horn, 134, 150
Trickeration, 106
Trouble Funk, 42, *56*, 56
T-Ski Valley, 46
Tuff City Records, 92, 119, 137, 148, 153
Tyrone Brunson, 146, 148

U Roy, 104
Universal Messengers, 79
UTFO, 122, 142

Vaughan Mason, 106
Ventures, 114
Vice Lord Nation, 58, 141
Vintertainment Records, 153

Wagadu-Gu, 114
War, 42, 45, 137
Warp 9, 146, 148, *150*, 150
Wayne and Charlie, *112*, 112
West Street Mob, 114
Whiz Kid, 107, 153
Whodini, 46, 122, 146
Wildstyle, 12, 36, 134
Willie 'The Lion' Smith, 22
Winley Records, 16, 83, 96–100, 108
Wood Brass and Steel, 105
World's Famous Supreme Team, 46, 134
Wuf Ticket, 8

Xanadu and Sweet Lady, 104

Yellow Magic Orchestra, 115, 129
Yellowman, 39
Younger Generation, 90

Zena Z, 93
Zulu, 57
Zulu Kings, 59
Zulu Nation, 57, 59, 133